Other books by Bob and Melinda Blanchard

A Trip to the Beach:
Living on Island Time in the Caribbean

At Blanchard's Table:
A Trip to the Beach Cookbook

Changing Your Course:
The 5-Step Guide to Getting the Life You Want

Cook What You Love:
Simple, Flavorful Recipes to Make Again and Again

Live What You Love ™

notes from a passionate life

Bob and Melinda Blanchard

STERLING

STERLING and the distinctive Sterling logo are registered trademarks of
Sterling Publishing Co., Inc.

Library of Congress Cataloging-in-Publication Data Available

2 4 6 8 10 9 7 5 3 1

Published by Sterling Publishing Co., Inc.
387 Park Avenue South, New York, NY 10016
© 2005, 2010 by Bob and Melinda Blanchard
Distributed in Canada by Sterling Publishing
c/o Canadian Manda Group, 165 Dufferin Street
Toronto, Ontario, Canada M6K 3H6
Distributed in the United Kingdom by GMC Distribution Services
Castle Place, 166 High Street, Lewes, East Sussex, England BN7 1XU
Distributed in Australia by Capricorn Link (Australia) Pty. Ltd.
P.O. Box 704, Windsor, NSW 2756, Australia

Live What You Love, LWYL, and
Blanchards are trademarks
of Bob and Melinda Blanchard.

Sterling ISBN 978-1-4027-2842-6 (hardcover)

Sterling ISBN 978-1-4027-7376-1 (paperback)

For information about custom editions, special sales, premium and
corporate purchases, please contact Sterling Special Sales
Department at 800-805-5489 or specialsales@sterlingpublishing.com.

Live What You Love ™

notes from a passionate life

A Note from Bob and Melinda

Living what we love all started about twenty-five years ago in Barbados. We were there with our five-year-old son Jesse and we'd spent the morning collecting shells and building sand castles. By lunchtime we were pretty hungry, but there wasn't a restaurant in sight.

We walked along the beach. After a mile or so, we spotted a picnic table, and nearby was a man leaning back on a lawn chair with his feet resting on a cooler and his face buried in a book. As we got closer, we saw a chalkboard sign propped against his chair. It read:

Hamburgers:	$10
Lobster:	$25
Beer & Soda:	$4

We stood in front of the man, who didn't acknowledge us until he had finished the page he was reading. Finally he looked up and asked, "Are you hungry?" We ordered three burgers and drinks and paid him our money, whereupon he opened his cooler and pulled out the drinks and three hamburgers. Three raw hamburgers. He handed us tongs and pointed to an oil drum that had been cut in half and turned into a charcoal grill.

That's when it dawned on us that we had just spent forty-two dollars for food that couldn't have cost our vendor more than five dollars. And we had to cook our own lunch.

We might have been annoyed had we not admired him so much. Why did we admire him? Because he didn't possess just a cooler of raw meat. He possessed an amazing ingenuity in bringing an idea to life—an idea we're pretty certain a lot of people had told him was crazy. He had come up with a simple business plan. He based his idea on the theory that people would either love to grill their own lunch on the beach or were hungry enough to do so. He found a location, researched the costs, and made his move. Mostly what he offered was a frame of mind and he was a living, breathing advertisement for the fact that there's more than one path to success. This man's ability to look at life a bit differently and create his own model for how to earn a living inspired us. He introduced to us a freedom that we'd never imagined possible. It was an "aha" moment for us; a moment that redefined our lives.

We've been called serial entrepreneurs. We've had nine businesses so far, half of which were started with less than $10,000. We're citizens of two countries: the United States and the Caribbean island of Anguilla. We're authors and builders.

We're restaurant owners and public speakers. We're married coworkers who like to say our life's work is building a life together. We live what we love.

But most of all, we follow our hearts. If we have an idea, we give it a shot. We're dreamers—big dreamers—and we've shaped our greatest dreams by will, not by whim. The will to live a life of passion and purpose. A life that strikes a balance between what's practical and what seems impossible. A life that doesn't fit neatly within the lines that others have drawn, but in the lines that we've drawn for ourselves.

Our life, admittedly, is not typical. It's unusual. And you know what? That makes it wonderful.

Living what you love means something different to all of us. For us, it's the independence of working for ourselves. For others, it's about moving closer to family, changing careers, or following a passion that just won't quit.

As you begin to sketch out what Live What You Love means to you, bear in mind that sometimes the experiences you have along the way matter as much as—or even more—than the outcome. They may not match your original expectations, but that's okay. In fact, it's more than okay. It's life.

What you treasure and remember—what lasts—is not expectations, and certainly not other people's expectations. It's about your experiences and what you do each and every day, and only you can decide what type of experiences are meaningful to you.

So shouldn't you live what you love? Go out and experience happiness, fulfillment, and greatness. Experience everything life has to offer.

LWYL,

Bob and Melinda Blanchard

Contents

Live What You Love ™

notes from a passionate life

Introduction: An Unusual Life

Living what you love is about gaining freedom and independence. It's about exploring your own direction in life and adopting an attitude that allows you to make your own decisions and manage more of your own time. Our world is in the throes of profound change and it matters now more than ever that we make meaningful life choices. The current state of the economy is bringing to light some long-overlooked truths as people recognize that the crisis we face involves far more than our finances. Who we are and what we care about are shifting, and although it's been a painful road for many, we believe there's a bright side. These uncertain financial times offer the opportunity to change and improve our everyday lives, and to confirm that optimism doesn't have to be a thing of the past. Now is the perfect time to reshape our lives into something richer, more sustainable, and more meaningful.

When we wrote our first book, *A Trip to the Beach*, the last thing we were expecting was fan mail. But we've been asked thousands of times, "How did you do it?" And people are not literally asking us the details of how we moved to Anguilla and opened a restaurant. They don't want to know about plane tickets or resorts—they're eager to know how we made such a life-changing decision to follow a dream. Weren't we terrified to take the risk? What obstacles did we overcome? Most importantly, what advice did we have to help them turn their own dreams into reality?

But nothing prepared us for what we call the "Katie Couric Moment." Going on the *Today* show for the first time was great in every way. Bright lights, lots of equipment, all those people watching while drinking their orange juice! We weren't even sure what to think or how to act. We were ready to tell a bit of our story about life in Anguilla—something practical, an interesting fact or two.

Then everything went silent. Katie Couric, the woman so

much of America admires, said to us on-air: "So my first question is . . . How can I be you?" What? How does Katie Couric get to be us? What was going on?

After reflecting on the fact that so many people wanted answers, we realized that what stood out most is that we had never said no to our dreams. We'd always examined where we were in life, and what we needed to do in order to continue on the path that was right for us. We balanced our dreams with practicalities, but never gave up on them. We were not afraid to risk it all and make huge mistakes, even if we had to start over again. We surrounded ourselves with people we love in places that nurture our souls. We made our dreams come true by living what we love every single day.

This book is our response to the thousands of people who continue to ask us for inspiration, advice, and encouragement. It's about following your heart and trusting your instincts. And it's for people at any stage of the game. People aren't born knowing how to multiply numbers, cook, or drive a car. We use flash cards, cookbooks, and driving lessons to teach us what we want to learn. People aren't born knowing how to live what they love either. *Live What You Love* is filled with stories about true life experiences. Those stories, in turn, offer advice, lessons, and many of the tools you'll need to take control of your own life. You'll learn quickly that there's no secret code or single solution to success. It's not what you chose to do that's important, but why and how you choose to do it.

Successfully living what you love means considering how to best weave the four major components of your life—passion, people, environment, and money—together in a way that makes sense for you. What's your passion? What activities energize you the most? Think about the people in your life. Do you look forward to seeing them each day? Does your environment make you feel positive and optimistic or do you long to be somewhere else? Then there's that prickly subject of money. Just remember that although money is certainly an essential element, it doesn't have to be the driving force in your decision to live what you love. You may be worried about your existing financial commitments or you might think that you don't have enough money to do whatever it is you'd like to do, but you'll see that there are always multiple ways to address these issues. Flexibility and hard work are key components.

We've made a life out of asking ourselves questions and making choices that allow us to bend and change as we move forward. And yet, there's nothing exceptional about us. If you've read our other books, you'll know how much we've struggled and how much we've had to learn along the way. We didn't know how to run a cookware store or start a gourmet food company until we tried. We certainly had no idea how to start a restaurant in a foreign country, or write a book, or create a line of products before we set out to try all three. We learned as we went, and we're grateful to be able to share all the lessons we've learned with you today.

Change of any kind is scary because you're dealing with the unknown. We believe that anyone can live a passionate, meaningful life. This book is not a comprehensive how-to guide, but rather a springboard to get you headed in the right direction. These passionate stories are what gave us strength and courage. They are the moments when our dreams were born, tested, and made real. Use our experiences—both our successes and failures—to look inside yourself and find your own courage.

We hope you enjoy them, and be sure to notice that our most successful ventures have been started in times of crisis. In fact, it's those difficult times that have forced us to learn new skills and adjust how we look at life. That's when we learn more about ourselves, and about how we want to live each and every day.

Be strong and hopeful. Never give up on your dreams and goals just because times are tough. Use bumps in the road as an opportunity to rethink exactly how you want to live and what you want to do. Now is the perfect time to take charge of your life. With the right vision, planning, and determination, anyone who wants to can live what they love. May you be blessed with a passionate life.

If your heart could speak,
what would it say?

no
experience necessary

Up to Our Ears in Cake Batter

Beginning a New Life

Recipe for a New Restaurant

From the early years when our son, Jesse, was born prematurely to the present when we get asked to share the joys of day-to-day life on national television, we've had a variety of unexpected experiences, experiences for which we were totally unprepared. But these experiences have taught us a great deal about life, passion, and meaning. They taught us the power of "amateur status." We didn't know we couldn't survive. We just pushed forward together, picking up each experience like a thread, unaware we were weaving a pattern.

Of course, this life that we love took some time and effort. We learned relatively quickly that experiences have a purpose. They can encourage us to take a careful look at how we are living; they can give us time to reflect; they can encourage us to make choices or take risks that can change our life. Whether it was the birth of our child, the starting of a business, or deciding to bake a cake, we saw that little experiences, little decisions, and little experiments can lead to big experiences, decisions, and lives. These, in turn, can and do lead to a more passionate, more meaningful life.

To some people, parts of our life might be considered ordinary or routine—anything but unusual. But each event was extraordinary for us. We assumed it would help us find some meaning or significance. We took the time to see each experience as an opportunity of a lifetime, as a chance to look at our life, and as a sign of meaning, structure, and significance in our life. Some experiences have been humbling; others have been fulfilling.

Each story here taught us to stop, to look, to read, and to examine what happens in our life. We learned that no experience is required to gain experience. We just had to live with our eyes wide open so we didn't miss a thing. ✴

Up to Our Ears in Cake Batter

August 2004

When a senior producer from the *Today* show called asking us if we'd be interested in making a wedding cake to use on the show, we might have said, "It's awfully nice of you to think of us, but I'm afraid we're just too busy." Or, I might have replied with complete candor, saying, "We've never made a wedding cake before; you'd probably be better off calling someone else." Instead, I answered impulsively, turning our lives upside down for the next two months. "Of course, we'd love to make a wedding cake for the show," I said. "Just let us know what you need and we'll deliver it to the studio whenever you like." After all, we run a successful restaurant, satisfying some pretty discerning tastes. Surely we could pull off a cake, right?

The annual *Today* show wedding series is an elaborate undertaking. Planning a wedding under ordinary circumstances is no easy task; pulling one together that will air on NBC for a show with ten million viewers requires an army of staff and the organizational skills of a five-star general. The *Today* show's audience votes to decide which couple from thousands of applicants will be chosen to marry on the air, as well as where the wedding will be held, what the invitations will look like, which gown the bride will wear, and all the other important details that go into planning a bride's dream wedding, including the cake!

This year, our little island of Anguilla became the destination of choice. We'd been on the show a number of times, and the producers naturally connected our names with Anguilla and called to invite us to bake one of the wedding cakes to be voted upon by the audience. The three other contestants were all professional cake decorators who had devoted years to the craft. Any one of them could make perfect sugar paste flowers with their eyes closed, and baking a two-foot-high, multi-tiered cake was almost an everyday event. We, on the other hand, didn't know what sugar paste was, much less how to shape it into tropical flowers and palm trees.

So, within twenty-four hours, we were studying all the

books on cake decorating we could find . . . and quickly realized we might have gotten in way over our heads. Each book expounded a different style, and they all had glossaries filled with words we didn't know, let alone understand. It also became clear that our well-equipped kitchen was not nearly as complete as we thought. Other than a Kitchen-Aid mixer, we had none of the equipment needed to make a cake of this scale.

But there was no turning back. We had promised the *Today* show we could make a cake and we were going to figure out how to do it. Mel disappeared into the kitchen to test cake recipes and I sequestered myself at my drafting table. I had no doubt about Mel's ability to produce a great-tasting cake; it was my design capabilities that frightened me. I've drawn house plans, restaurant plans, boat plans, and plans for retail stores, but when the *Today* show asked for a rendering of our wedding cake, I didn't know where to begin.

I sat at my drawing board studying books and sharpening pencils for two days before an idea hit me. There was no way we could compete with the pros by making a traditional cake. We had to be creative. I had already spent hours trying to make an edible bougainvillea flower petal, only to realize that professionals go to school to learn that sort of thing. I pictured our cake on national television with millions of people wondering what these amateurs were doing on the show. I was pretty sure it would be our last appearance on NBC.

I shared my fears with Mel and she agreed. "Why would we want to make the same cake everyone else makes?" she asked. "The world doesn't need another white cake with seashells and flowers. We're from Anguilla and our cake should tell a story. It should show viewers what Anguilla is all about."

I thought about her idea, knowing she was right. Our biggest advantage over all the other bakers was our tie to Anguilla. Perhaps the other bakers had looked it up on a map, but we'd lived on this remarkable little island for over a decade. We knew the people and understood their customs. This wedding wouldn't just take place on a beach, it would be on a beach in Anguilla. I began drawing.

Meanwhile, Mel baked. She tested dozens of recipes: white cakes, yellow cakes, and chocolate cakes; glazes, buttercream icings, fondant coverings; and fillings, creams, and meringues. The list was endless.

Our cake, we finally decided, would be a gift to Nikki and Buddy, the bride and groom. They knew nothing about Anguilla and we wanted to give them something that represented the island, something personal. Each buttercream-filled layer would represent a different aspect of island life.

As we began to accumulate equipment. Cake pans ranging in size from four to sixteen inches covered the dining room table. Sets of decorating tips along with pastry bags, rolling pins, leaf cutters, flower molds, and cutting tools arrived by FedEx daily. I came downstairs one morning to find that Mel had already cleaned out the refrigerator, gone grocery shopping, and thrown out all the leftover Chinese food, as well as my favorite sandwich ingredients. Butter and eggs were all that remained. Fifty pounds of butter and twenty-four dozen eggs.

"What did you do with my beer?" I asked, staring into the refrigerator. "And where's the milk for my coffee?"

"It's in the garage," Mel answered, waving hands pink from the colored fondant. The pink looked permanent to me.

"I can't get the color right on these beach chairs. It's either too pink or too red." Shifting to the other side of the kitchen counter, she continued, "What do you think of this blue for the beach umbrellas?" She held up a ball of blue fondant sealed with plastic wrap to keep it moist.

"It's perfect," I said. "But how are we going to *make* the umbrellas?"

"I was hoping you could figure that out," she said with a smile. "You're the engineer."

"I think I'd better call Sue," I replied. "I bet she'll know what to do. I have no idea how to stick the top of the umbrella onto the pole without using Elmer's glue. And I know that's against the rules, right?"

"No glue," Mel agreed. "Everything has to be edible."

Sue Chandler owns a cake decorating store in Concord, New Hampshire, about sixty miles away from our home in Vermont. We'd purchased most of our baking paraphernalia from Sue's shop and realized immediately that Sue was a cake goddess. She knew everything. And lucky for us, she would enthusiastically answer any of our questions morning, noon, or night. Two hours after calling Sue, we were seated in her back room, taking a private lesson in sugar paste decoration. It reminded me of making Play-Doh dinosaurs with Jesse when he was little, but we came away with extensive knowledge of sugar and fully prepared to produce beach umbrellas, seashells, and sailboats.

As our decorating skills improved and our cake began to take shape, the story we were trying to tell with each layer became clearer. The bottom tier represented the pale turquoise water of the Caribbean, which we would cover with edible coral and seashells. The second tier depicted an Anguilla boat race and would be decorated with chocolate and sugar sailboats gliding around the island. The next tier was designed to showcase Anguilla's powdery white sand beaches and was adorned with chairs, umbrellas, and tropical foliage. On top of everything we placed a traditional Caribbean cottage, complete with white picket fence, red tin roof, and wooden shutters—all edible, of course—to represent Nikki and Buddy's new life together.

Boat racing is the national sport of Anguilla and is very serious business. Thousands of people turn out to watch boat races; the winning captains are local folk heroes. The boats are handmade wooden craft with gigantic sails and hold crews of fourteen, some of whom are used for ballast. Each one is built in a different village, and entire communities often help with construction. We planned to explain the importance of Anguilla boat racing on the *Today* show because it was such an integral part of our cake design.

As the deadline approached, the wedding cake began taking over more and more of our lives. We'd made enough miniature beach chairs to cover twenty cakes, and although our skills were improving every day, it was still hard to get exactly the size, look, color, and proportion we wanted. If we rolled out the sugar paste too thin, it became fragile. Too thick, and it looked like a third-grade school project. We piped chocolate coral onto parchment paper in various shapes and traced photos of Anguilla sails onto rolled sheets of white sugar paste. We drove for miles in search of tiny toy boats to use as molds and scouted for just the right tool to make a corrugated "tin" roof.

We discovered the hard way that slicing cake layers evenly and filling them with buttercream isn't so easy either. We struggled to get the first nine layers smooth and level until we were satisfied that they were just right. Unfortunately, when we placed the first three-layered little cottage of happiness on top, it tilted precariously, looking as if it had survived a mudslide. For one brief, fleeting moment, we considered hiring Sue to make the cake for us. But we knew that would be cheating. Besides, once we'd come this far, we weren't the sort to give up.

We pulled an all-nighter the day before the cake was due. The finished cake was iced and chilling in the refrigerator by three in the afternoon. Things were under control. Several hours later, we opened the refrigerator and, to our horror, discovered that temperature affects the color of buttercream. Our turquoise Caribbean looked more like the Black Sea, and the pale pink cottage looked suspiciously like a fire engine.

Meanwhile the cake had to be at the studio in New York by noon the next day, which meant we had to leave our house in Vermont at five o'clock in the morning. Mel and I stood in front of the refrigerator staring dumbly at our cake's new dark colors. We began again. By midnight we were on icing batch number twenty, and by 4:00 a.m. our kitchen looked as if a multicolored bomb had exploded.

We drove away from the remains of our baking marathon just as the sun was coming up with the cake safely stored in an insulated box with our car's air conditioner blasting. Sue had warned us about the perils of transporting wedding cakes, and she'd shared enough horror stories that we paid close attention. We drove slowly, trying to stay away from other cars and cursing every bump in the road.

As Mel and I placed the finishing touches on our wedding cake in the back room of the *Today* show's studio, we eyed the three other cake entries for the first time. They were beautiful. One was completely covered with real seashells; another was made from cookies and stood nearly three feet tall. The third, we learned, had been flown in from California.

My mind wandered back over the past two months and I pictured the pile of cake decorating books in our kitchen, now dog-eared and covered with icing. I thought of the countless trips to Sue and all the tutorials she'd generously given us. I couldn't believe we'd gotten this far. We'd made a cake that would make Anguilla proud, and that meant more to us than winning.

In the end our cake was not chosen as the winner. But do we regret the experience? Not for one minute. We knew the entire population of our island would be watching the show, cheering for our cake just as if it were a real boat in a real race.

Beginning a New Life

March 1974

We're lucky. We've thought a lot about our life and how we managed to end up where we are today. When did it really begin to take shape? Were we guided by fate or smart enough to have had a plan?

Our story began in a hospital room in 1974 when we were both in our early twenties, and like many life changes ours began in crisis. This crisis, we would later discover, was the starting point of our journey. It was to be the defining moment of our life when we were forced to take stock, figure out where we were, and begin shaping our future. It was terrifying. As we said, we're lucky.

It was the middle of the night and the two of us were alone in a gray hospital waiting room. The voice of Kathy Albright, one of the ICU nurses, crackled harshly through the speaker: "Melinda, you and Bob can come in now." I watched, numb, as Mel got up, walked across the cold tile floor, pushed the intercom button, and in a weak voice replied, "Okay."

Together we crossed the hall, punched the automatic door opener and stared as a pair of heavy metal doors hissed outward like the open jaws of some mythical beast, ready to swallow anyone or anything daring to enter. Shaking, we walked through the unwelcoming doors and into the pediatric ward ICU prep room, where we donned green hospital johnnies, white caps, and scrubbed up with brown disinfectant.

We tried hard to ignore the grim sounds of respirators, beeping monitors, and crying relatives as we followed Kathy toward our tiny new son. Mel squeezed my hand hard enough to hurt. Finally we reached Jesse's incubator and were able to see our brave and precious newborn baby.

Weighing only one pound, ten ounces, Jesse had been given less than a 4 percent chance of taking his first breath. Not only had he beaten those odds, Jesse had entered life kicking and screaming. The nurses said he had an extraordinary will to live; we called him our miracle.

The doctors were more cautious, warning us not to raise our hopes too high. "He has many hurdles to get over," Dr. George Little, the head of neonatology, explained, "all of which are complicated by PDA, or patent ductus arteriosus, which is a periodical malfunction of the heart that manifests itself as a murmur. We've scheduled him for surgery tomorrow afternoon and we'll do our best—but his chances of survival are still very, very slim."

"So why operate?" I asked.

"Each time Jesse's heart malfunctions blood flow into the brain is diminished, placing Jesse in severe danger. If we're successful, surgery will at least eliminate that risk. I'll need your consent to operate, but don't feel that you have to make this decision alone. We'll sit down together and make our decision in the morning. Right now, I want you two to go home and get some rest."

When Dr. Little left, I hugged Mel and, our eyes wet with tears, we stood over Jesse's incubator in silent vigil, gazing at our beautiful son lying on his inhuman bed of tubes and wires, fighting for his life. Mel broke the silence, mumbling, "This is not a decision any parent should ever have to make."

We spent that night in the hospital. Each time Jesse's heart monitor straight-lined, an alarm would sound, bringing a team of doctors and nurses charging to his side. The night seemed endless, and we lost all track of time. At 8:30 a.m. we were still waiting for signs of improvement, hoping to be spared having to decide our child's fate. On top of everything else, I was again late for work and Mel was missing yet another day of classes.

"I don't know if I can get off from work again today," I said, "and I may very well get fired over this. I've already missed two and a half weeks and I'm afraid the State of Vermont won't have much sympathy." I was working for a social service program at the time and though I needed to get back to my clients, I was too tired to call my supervisor. We continued to wait in silence.

Finally Mel spoke up. "If the three of us ever get out of this place, I think you should find another way to earn a living. I can't imagine all of us not being together every day. There's no way I'm going to work, waiting until evening to spend time with you and Jesse." I wasn't sure what she meant by that remark but I sensed it was important.

Dr. Little found us in the waiting room still undecided about Jesse's surgery. "Good news," he said, smiling. "Jesse's done it again. Proved us wrong, I mean. His heart murmur seems to have stopped. He's an amazing little guy. Have you two been here all night?"

"Yeah, I guess we have," I said.

"We both thought it might be his last night," Mel said.

"Why don't you go home and get some rest?" Dr. Little said. "I'll call you if anything changes."

We made our way downstairs and out into the bright sunshine and crisp air of an early April morning. The trip home took us nearly two hours and we drove it in silence, lost in thought.

Over the next two months we got to know that road well as we drove back and forth to visit Jesse. He was growing steadily. And so was as his hospital bill. We had no medical insurance and no idea how we would ever pay what we knew would be an overwhelming amount of money.

The day Jesse was discharged, he weighed a whopping four pounds, five ounces and the bill was six times my annual salary. Nervously, we sat in the business office waiting to discuss payment with the hospital's administrators. I assumed they would simply garnish my wages for the rest of my life. Finally the door opened and Dr. Little walked in, followed by three men in suits. *The money guys,* I said to myself.

"First of all, we'd like to thank you for your help during Jesse's stay," Dr. Little began. Mel and I looked at each other, not knowing what to say. What on earth were they thanking *us* for?

"Dartmouth is a teaching hospital but we can't teach without the help of our patients. Thanks to your unconditional support and cooperation, we've been able to learn a tremendous amount from Jesse's birth and the first ten weeks of his life."

"You were all so compassionate," Mel blurted out, "we couldn't imagine going through this anywhere else. We would do anything for you."

"Well," Dr. Little continued, "we have some good news for you. We understand that the bill far exceeds what you can afford. The hospital has decided to pick up the tab. You don't owe us a thing."

Overcome by emotion, we sat staring. Dr. Little broke the silence. "Let's go upstairs and get Jesse so you can take him home. We'll want to see him regularly for a while, so you're not done with us yet. But right now it's time to get the three of you home."

"You're kidding, right?" I finally managed. "About the bill, I mean. We don't owe anything at all?" Dr. Little just smiled and motioned for us to follow. We struggled to find words to express our relief and gratitude, but none came. Even after thirty years the magnitude of how that moment changed our lives is still hard for us to comprehend.

We hugged the staff from the ICU who had walked to the car with us. Dr. Little was there, along with the head nurses, Kathy Albright and Linda Brown. Jesse was the only one not crying.

And that was it. We weren't about to take a single moment of this life for granted. We knew what love could do, and we were going to live smack in the middle of it.

Recipe for a New Restaurant
January 1994

I love to design and build things. Ever since I was old enough to carry a hammer around with me, I was happiest when I was creating something. It didn't matter what it was as long as I could draw a picture, figure out how to make it, and then build it.

I built a twenty-four-foot pontoon boat when I was eleven and a go-kart with a V-4 engine and four-speed transmission when I was thirteen. It topped out at eighty miles per hour and my poor parents knew they had their hands full, especially when I took one of my mother's dining room chairs, cut the legs off, and used it for the seat. My father wanted me to be an architect or an engineer and my mother wanted me to study literature and be a professor. I just wanted to build things.

When Mel and I found ourselves getting ready to open our restaurant on the island of Anguilla, it was the perfect use of my passion for design. The restaurant had to be warm, comfortable, casual, elegant, and timeless all at the same time, and it would take considerable planning before we could start building. The best spot, we concluded, to design such a place was under a blue umbrella on the beach in front of our future restaurant.

"What colors should we use?" I asked as I began to sketch various floor plans.

"I think Caribbean teal against a clean white background would be beautiful. Take the color of the sea and bring it into the restaurant."

"We need to make it feel open and airy during dinner, yet be able to close it up at night," I said. "I'm thinking shutters all the way around. We could paint them the color of the water and make the walls white."

"And we need ceiling fans to cool it down on hot nights," Mel added. She closed her eyes and dug her toes into the sand. "We could use white chairs with cushions that match the shutters. Keep it very simple."

"I'd like to accent it with some natural mahogany," I said. "A mahogany bar and a few other small touches here and there would warm it up a bit. And I see crisp white tablecloths with candles and tropical flowers. And tall, thin-stemmed wine-glasses. Do you remember the wine cellar at Georges Blanc in France?"

"Yes," Mel said. "The walls were floor-to-ceiling glass and you could see all the wine, right?"

"That's right." I was picturing a ninety-thousand-bottle cellar with three thousand selections. "We can't afford one that big, but we could have a respectable cellar and make it visible from the dining room. I think it would be spectacular and sell more wine, too."

"That sounds great as long as we don't have the pretentious formality that usually comes with an impressive wine collection. The fun part would be to offer a great selection of wine, unsurpassed service, and fresh, creatively prepared food in a surprisingly casual atmosphere."

I began to draw with purpose. Mel closed her eyes, soaking up the warmth, waiting for my rendering.

"How about this?" I held up my rough floor plan for her to see.

"I think you should keep working on it," she said. "Put some more corners in it so it's not just a rectangle. We need to have a few nooks and crannies."

As we talked, I kept drawing new ideas.

33

"I want to be careful about not making the waitstaff uniforms too formal," Mel said. "We have to remember that people come to the Caribbean to relax. I can't stand when we go to a place with great food down here and the waiter comes over in formal black and white with necktie—or worse yet, a bow tie. Some of them even wear jackets. How can you expect people to unwind when they're surrounded by stuffy men dressed like they're in a three-star restaurant in Paris?"

The sun was dropping lower in the sky. Now out of the shade, my legs were getting a little hot. "I'm going for a swim," I announced.

"I'm staying right here," Mel said. "Think about the garden while you're swimming. It needs a focal point."

I floated along with the gentle waves for a while, dreaming of teal shutters and romantic tables with flickering candles and tiny vases filled with pink bougainvillea. My mind wandered through lush gardens reaching down to the sea and whitewashed steps descending to the beach.

"How about fountains?" I asked as I toweled off.

"Sorry, I guess I dozed off," Mel said. "Fountains?"

"You said you wanted a focal point in the gardens. Fountains would be great."

"That's perfect." Mel sat up. "How do you build fountains?"

"I don't know but we'll figure it out," I said. "I'll go to a plumbing store or a landscape place when we go up north. I'm sure there are books on how to build fountains, too. I bet Home Depot has everything to spray water in any shape or as high as we want."

"We need to create a feeling of serenity. Fountains are peaceful. I love it," Mel said. "I've also been picturing a picket fence out front. It would make it feel like a cottage. What do you think?"

"I don't want it to be too much like New England," I answered, settling down in my beach chair. "But if we cover the fence with tropical foliage and surround it with palms, it will be beautiful."

"Okay, so here's what we've got." Mel was reading from one of her never-ending lists. "Teal and white, shutters everywhere, gardens and fountains, candlelit tables, great wine cellar, mahogany bar, and a picket fence covered with flowers. Oh, and I'm adding that all the lights should be on dimmers so we can control the mood. Did I miss anything?"

"Food?" I asked with a smile. "And a staff to make all this happen."

"You take care of the construction and the wine and I'll come up with the menu," Mel said. "The food will be simple but full of flavor. Nothing too fussy, just great combinations of taste, color, and texture. Lots of fresh vegetables and of course plenty of seafood. We'll have to test some recipes pretty soon. I can't wait to start grilling some local lobsters. As far as the staff goes, I think we should use our usual philosophy of not hiring people with too much experience. They always come with bad habits. What we need is enthusiasm. We have to find people who want to learn how to create a perfect environment."

The sun was sinking below the horizon on Meads Bay, and the idea of testing recipes was sounding very good. "I'm hungry," I said. "Let's try grilling some lobster right now."

We packed up our beach chairs and umbrella and went off to find some lobster. Blanchard's was coming together, and we knew that opening night would be like the curtain going up on stage. The restaurant would be the set and the staff, the players.

Remember

Do

Live like you mean it.

Believe that life is to be lived and loved.

Follow your heart.

Don't

Take a single moment for granted.

Think you have to take everyone's advice.

Allow your fear to paralyze you.

Imagine living your entire life only to realize that what seemed to be important . . .

really wasn't so
urgent after all.

the big **4**

Peanie and the '49 Dodge

We Love Food

Where Is Carlye?

Beginnings are exciting. We dream of what will spring from our imaginations, off the stove, into the marketplace, and into our lives. We can almost taste its sweet success—whether it's a new recipe, a new building, a new business, or a new life. Along with the joy, excitement, and anticipation comes the challenge. How do we do this? How do we make *this* dream a reality? How do we take everything we've learned and use it to our advantage?

Drawing from experience, we've identified four checkpoints in life that help us connect our dreams with reality. We affectionately call these checkpoints the Big 4: PASSION, PEOPLE, ENVIRONMENT, and MONEY, and, like the pistons in your car engine, they should all be in proper working order and running smoothly. We've always tried to live life guided by our passions, surrounded by people we love, and living in places we enjoy. We try not to put more emphasis on any one of the Big 4—they're all important—although we feel strongly that money should always come last. Money's primary function is to make the other three possible.

The experience of starting eight business ventures over more than thirty years has also taught us to periodically evaluate our lives even as we're living our dream. Do we have the skills, the abilities, and the resources to make the dream fulfilling and keep it sustained? Is this the *place* where we want to be? Are these the *people* with whom we wish to share our life? Do we believe in what we are doing? Are we *passionate* about it? Are we moving toward a life we love? You need to be honest with yourself, your expectations, and your experience if you want to live what you love. Even though your dreams are strong, you shouldn't be afraid to check them against reality. We do this all the time.

There's really only
one way to learn how
to do something:
You have to do it.

Peanie and the '49 Dodge

February 1976

In 1976 I was a social worker earning six thousand dollars a year. Mel's father had just left her eight thousand dollars, a small fortune at the time, and we thought we were rich. So we agreed that I'd quit my job and we'd use our new fortune to buy a business. We were desperate to work together, and running our own business seemed like our best option. I'd grown up working in my father's Vermont general store, and Mel and I decided to look for one that we could buy and run ourselves. We called several real estate brokers and asked them to scour Vermont for the general store of our dreams.

We owned a twenty-seven-year-old, mint-condition 1949 Dodge at the time, which I'd bought off a dealer's showroom floor. Since it had been built well before the days of safety regulations, we'd installed a seat belt in the back to secure Jesse's car seat. Our '49 Dodge attracted lots of attention and every broker insisted on riding with us when we drove around to look at general stores.

Our search went on and on, and we soon began to realize that there were two flaws in our otherwise perfect plan. The first was cost. Most of the stores included real estate, often an owner's apartment, and many came with several acres of prime commercial land. Our eight thousand dollars wouldn't even cover the down payment. The second flaw was revenue. We were shocked at how little money each store made, and most of the general stores we looked at were forced to stay open seven days a week to compete with the mini-marts that were popping up like weeds all across the state. Even if we could find a bank willing to give us financing, we would use all our profits to pay off debt while we worked sixteen-hour days and seven-day weeks for little more than food and shelter.

While brokers were content riding around in the back of our '49 Dodge showing us things we couldn't afford, we were quickly losing interest. So they started showing us businesses more within our budget—and we became even more frustrated. We looked at a nasty little convenience store in Windsor that mainly sold beer and cigarettes and was listed at fifty thousand dollars. The broker said the owner would take less and might even offer financing. He was very anxious to sell. I could see why.

We looked at an abandoned A&W drive-up that could be brought back to life for a mere forty-two thousand, but when the broker pointed to a rusting green mobile home in back where the owners were expected to live, Mel refused to even get out of the car. "I'm not flipping burgers in that greasy kitchen— and just picture yourself in a brown-and-orange car-hop uniform, serving root beer to giggling teenagers in the parking lot," she remarked.

"It doesn't have to be an A&W," the broker said, trying to be helpful. "You could open any kind of restaurant here. This town could really use a good pancake house." He was full of great ideas.

"Let's go," Mel said, patience wearing thin.

The next day we were shown what was described as a "curio shoppe" on the main street of Montpelier. It was a leased space with no real estate and was priced at thirty-five thousand.

The broker enthusiastically told us that the owner was willing to finance everything if we used our eight thousand dollars as the down payment. We decided to study the books.

The "shoppe" records showed the owners claiming seven thousand dollars' worth of inventory and ten thousand dollars' worth of fixtures. The balance was listed as the value of the trade name, customer goodwill, and favorable long-term lease. The bottom line showed current profits of roughly twelve thousand dollars a year, which would allow us to take six thousand dollars in income and use the rest to pay off debt. It seemed feasible.

"What do you think?" I asked Mel on our drive home. "It's not exactly what we had in mind but it could work."

"I'd want to get rid of some of the inventory," Mel answered. "I mean, the figurine collection and the pewter candlesticks would have to go. And do you really want to sell mugs that say KISS THE COOK? And what exactly is a 'curio' anyway?"

"I'd want to replace most of the display fixtures, too," I added. "It's very dark inside. We could pull all the gray barn boards from the walls and put up new, light-colored pine or spruce. We need to brighten it up."

We drove along in silence for a bit, thankful that Jesse was as content in his car seat as he was almost anywhere else. He looked happy holding his tattered yellow blanket and watching the scenery fly by, unaware that his parents were about to plunk down their once-in-a-lifetime nest egg to purchase a curio shoppe.

"Listen," I began, "if we're going to get rid of the inventory, change the decor, and build all new displays, what are we actually paying for? The trade name wouldn't be worth anything since we'd end up with a completely different store. The curio customers probably won't like it, so even the customer goodwill is worthless."

"Just what I was thinking." Mel smiled. "You know what we should do?"

"I think we should just start from scratch," I said.

"Exactly!" Mel was getting excited now. "Let's find a space to rent and open a store filled with things we love."

One morning we saw an ad in the real estate section of our local paper that read, "Colonial Plaza; new shopping center; space for lease." We put Jesse in his car seat and set off to take a look. We weren't sure what we were looking for but we knew we'd seen more than enough A&Ws and convenience stores. *Maybe, just maybe,* we each thought, *today will be our lucky day.*

The Colonial Plaza is located in the middle of a growing retail sprawl in New Hampshire, just across the border from Vermont. New Hampshire has no sales tax, making it a big draw for customers from neighboring states.

We drove our '49 Dodge into the plaza's parking lot and were greeted by an exuberant landlord who introduced himself as Peanie Goodwin. Peanie was a logger and dressed the part. He wore red-and-black-checkered wool pants held up by orange suspenders, a flannel shirt, and a wool cap with earflaps down. "Nice cah," he said, strolling around the Dodge. "Fohty-eight or fohty-nine?"

"Forty-nine," I answered. "We came to look at the space for lease."

"You wanna sell that cah?" Peanie squared off in front of me, hooking his thumbs in his suspenders.

"No," I answered. "We saw an ad in the paper about space for lease. Is this it?"

"Yep," he replied, gesturing toward the new building where a roofing crew was busy slapping shingles over fresh tarpaper. "I'm almost finished and it's just about fully leased. I've got a coupla stores left. What kinda store you wanna open?" He rocked on the heels of his rubber boots as he readjusted his suspenders.

"We're not exactly sure," I replied, "but we'll sell nice gifts and things for the home." It was a lame answer but we hadn't totally thought this through.

Mel jumped in, saying, "I'm thinking about cookware and dinnerware."

I stared at her in disbelief. Where did she get that idea?

"You mean pots and pans?" Peanie seemed to glare at her, and I could feel this conversation heading south. He could tell she was from New York. I held my breath.

"You know, young lady." Peanie had by now turned his back on me, positioning himself between us, and I was expecting the worst. "I can't find a decent cast-iron fry pan 'roun' here anywhere. You gonna carry heavy pots and pans like that? You know, the old-fashion kind?"

"That's what we were thinking," Mel answered.

I hadn't been thinking this at all, but it wasn't a bad idea. Of course, I would have bought the A&W.

"Let's look at the space," Peanie said. He unlocked the door and we went in. It was eight hundred square feet, carpeted and Sheetrocked, with a tiny bathroom in the back. The space was just aching to be filled with cast-iron pots and pans.

"How much is the rent?" I asked.

"Six hundred a month and you pay the heat and electric," Peanie answered.

"And how long is the lease?" I asked.

"Look," Peanie began, "I don't like lawyers and I don't like leases. You pay me the six hundred dollars a month, don't do anything illegal in here, and we'll get along just fine. If you don't like it, you can leave. If you don't pay me the rent or if you turn out to be a pain in the neck, I'm gonna kick you out. That sound fair?"

"Sounds fair to me," Mel said.

We went outside, and Peanie eyed the Dodge once more. "You ever wanna sell that cah—you call me," he said. "If you want, the space is yours. I'll hold it 'til tomorrow."

We drove away feeling as if we'd just hit the jackpot.

"It's perfect," Mel began. "There's no lease so we're not locked in to anything. And we're not paying for inventory we don't want and fixtures we don't need. We'll just buy the stuff we like, and once you build shelves and we've set up displays, we can move in."

We went home and turned over all our cookware and dishes. "This one says Le Creuset," I said, "and the teakettle is made by Copco. Your favorite dishes say ARABIA—MADE IN FINLAND. How on earth would we locate that?"

"I have no idea," Mel replied. "Let's call information in New York. I think everyone has an office in New York."

The first company we asked for was Copco, and sure enough, they had a number in New York.

"Where are you located?" the woman asked.

"Vermont," Mel answered.

"Our sales rep for your area is located in Boston. Give me your number and I'll have him give you a call."

In fact, we had hit the jackpot. Within a few weeks sales reps from all over New England were coming to see us. They were eager to have their goods placed in our store and offered us promotions, special pricing, and all kinds of deals. We quickly learned that you can buy most products wholesale with just a business card and shipping address. Before we knew it, our little apartment was filled with boxes containing cookware, dishes, glasses, table linens, and kitchen accessories of every sort imaginable.

Who knew that this first little business would spark a lifetime of entrepreneurial adventure?

We Love Food

Long before I'd met Bob, my mom brought me to the World's Fair in New York. I still remember the Belgian waffle I ate at the fair when I was twelve years old. It was warm with a soft center and crispy edges and piled high with cold, freshly cut strawberries, smothered with spoonfuls of smooth, not overly-sweetened whipped cream. Ask me what else I remember about the World's Fair and I draw a complete blank. Did I have a good time? Absolutely; that waffle was perfect. I had an inkling then that my priorities were not necessarily the same as those of the people around me.

That same year, when I was in seventh grade, I mistakenly thought that because I loved grammar and books, my English teacher was a friend. I thought we had an understanding: She'd ask the class a question and I'd enthusiastically raise my hand, hoping to provide the answer. We were at peace with each other. And then, from out of the blue, with the announcement of a single homework assignment, my friendly teacher turned hostile.

"Class," she began, "I'd like you each to prepare a speech for next Monday."

My immediate response was to schedule a doctor's appointment on Monday. No class, no speech.

"I want you to have fun with this assignment," she continued. "You can talk about anything you like."

Fun? I thought. *Who is she kidding?*

During lunch, I listened in horror as my classmates shared ideas about speech topics. Panicked beyond belief, I excused myself and went home early after complaining to the school nurse about pains in my stomach. They were real.

My mother didn't seem to understand my fear of speeches. "You talk nonstop," she said. "What's the big deal about talking in front of your class? Just choose a subject that interests you and you'll be fine."

"That's what the teacher said," I answered, not convinced.

Putting the horror of public speaking aside, I distracted myself by heading for the kitchen. I peeled a bowl full of hard-boiled eggs, carefully removing the yolks. I mashed the yolks with mustard, mayonnaise, a little white wine vinegar, and a few drops of Tabasco sauce.

I used a rubber spatula to blend the mixture, adding a little salt and pepper to taste. By the time I finished testing and seasoning, the creamy, slightly spicy filling was both comforting and enlightening. My mind wandered back to the school lunchroom where my friends were debating whether they should speak about politics, civil rights, or Vietnam. I had a brainstorm. My seventh-grade class was about to learn how to make deviled eggs.

Though my teacher was surprised when I arrived on speech day with mixing bowls, kitchen utensils, and a cooler, my presentation was a hit. I explained the intricacies of mashing, seasoning, filling, and decorating the eggs and passed around samples for the class. The girl whose speech followed mine was the ninth student to talk about politics and world events. The yawns were audible even as she began.

When I lived in New York, I spent weekends and school vacations at a ski camp in Vermont. Though other kids often helped prepare dinner, I was drawn to the kitchen as if pulled by a giant magnet. And though skiing was ostensibly the reason I was there in the first place, my memories are more of cooking than zooming down the slopes.

One Saturday over Christmas vacation I intentionally missed the bus that took everyone up to the mountain. I had another plan for the day. Several weeks earlier I'd watched Julia Child prepare chocolate éclairs on television. I've always loved a good éclair and was eager to try making my own. I raided the kitchen at camp and pulled out enough butter, sugar, eggs, flour, cream, and chocolate to make two hundred éclairs. Looking back, I can't figure out why I didn't attempt such a complicated recipe in the privacy of my own home.

Not surprisingly, the ski camp kitchen was not equipped with the pastry bag called for in the recipe, so once I perfected the dough, I used a spoon to shape four-inch-long oblongs onto every sheet pan I could find. Rows of éclairs covered every surface in the kitchen, spilling out to the dining room by the time I was done. It took me all day to complete the project; I was filling and glazing the last few pastries just as everyone was coming back from the slopes. Perfect timing. A typical dessert at camp was a slice from a block of tricolored Neapolitan ice cream. Needless to say, my éclairs were a welcome treat. I wanted to call Julia and tell her about my success.

One of the most common questions I'm asked in the restaurant is, "Where were you trained?" When I explain that I'm self-taught and probably wouldn't have the patience to attend culinary school, the next question is inevitably, "Have you always loved to cook?" I think back to the days of Belgian waffles, deviled eggs, and éclairs and respond with a simple yes. I doubt customers would be impressed by the simplicity of my so-called training.

My greatest passion is and always has been food. Most recently cookbooks have been our latest outlet for creating new recipes. Bob tests each one on his own, ensuring that they're easy and really work the way they should.

"Mel, come taste this while it's still warm," Bob yelled from the kitchen.

"Coming," I called.

Two minutes passed and he tried again. "Mel, come on," he urged, "you won't believe how good this bread pudding is. This time it's perfect."

"Okay, okay. I'll be right there," I answered.

After a few more minutes, he took matters into his own hands, appearing alongside my desk holding a huge bowl filled with warm chocolate bread pudding. "You're going to love this," he said, as he loaded up a giant spoonful to bring to my mouth.

"Oh, wow!" I moaned. "This is great. Much better than the last batch." I pulled off some of the crispy chocolate on top and dipped it into the smooth, creamy pudding underneath.

"Let's make sure we get a photograph of this for the book," I said. "It should be a close-up shot." Bob spooned another large portion into my mouth. I didn't refuse.

"Mmmm" was about all I could say.

"I'm going to try the Reggae Pork and Mexican Mashed Potatoes now," he said enthusiastically.

Bob loves testing recipes. He can cook all day long and never tire. "Just don't put me in the restaurant kitchen," he insists. "There's too much pressure in there."

An hour or so later he came back to my desk carrying two large plates of food, each with generous portions of pork marinated in lime, guava, and rum. It was a fantastic dish, exploding with island flavor. Bob had arranged the pork over potatoes that were mashed with Vermont cheddar cheese and had a subtle kick thanks to cilantro and assorted chilies. As if that wasn't enough food at eleven o'clock in the morning, he'd also made the Caesar Coleslaw I'd suggested the day before. We finished eating everything on our plates, marveling at how much fun it was getting paid to eat.

After two weeks we'd tested and tasted nearly forty recipes to use in our new cookbook. Things were going very well, but I was beginning to worry: I'd gained six pounds, and six pounds is no joke. Our cookbook would have one hundred recipes, and at this rate I'd gain fifteen pounds before we even finished testing.

"I sure hope you still love me when I'm as big as a hippopotamus," I said, only half kidding.

Bob laughed and gave me a big hug. "Let's go out for dinner tonight. We really should try that new bistro in town. Market research, you know."

Where Is  Carlye?

July 1987

In its early days, our specialty food business, Blanchard & Blanchard, was run entirely out of our house. Even though we'd all but lost the use of our kitchen, except for family dinners, and we couldn't use our dining room because it had become the shipping area, we were truly happy running a cottage industry out of our very own cottage. Mel was able to make fudge sauce all morning without leaving home, while I packed orders for Bloomingdale's and Macy's with the Rolling Stones blasting from the stereo. Curious friends and neighbors stopped by nearly every day to help out. We often worked well past midnight making batch after batch of Lemon-Pepper Vinaigrette and Horseradish Mustard.

Jesse helped after school and became "Master of Sealing Salad Dressing Caps" by the time he was nine years old, having figured out the benefits of a production line by recruiting friends to help. David Cook worked to his right, handing him caps, with Patrick Albertini to his left lining up bottles to ready them for labeling. Soon they could hold their own against any respectable conveyer belt assembly line.

Our first official employee was David's mother, Carlye, and we were delighted that she'd joined our little business. She was happy to tackle any job and was always willing to work late into the evening, as long as she could bring David along. Our house slowly turned into a community center, and we loved it. It smelled like oil and vinegar from Monday through Wednesday, mustard on Thursday and Friday, and chocolate on the weekends.

A joyful spirit permeated our house in those days, energizing everyone who came to help. They all applauded anytime a new account called to place an order. "We just opened Neiman Marcus," Mel would announce after hanging up the phone. Or, "Hay Day just reordered. They say our dressing is flying off the shelves!" Our company was growing quickly.

But as much as we loved seeing our little business grow, we

struggled to keep up with the pace. "We need bigger mixing tanks," I said, "and we should start buying in bulk."

"I know," Mel said, "but where do we put bigger tanks? Just look at this place!" I stopped stirring mustard for a minute, taking stock of our kitchen. It was so full of stockpots, blenders, and mixers that there was no counter space left. The stove was covered with double boilers, while cases of bottles were piled all over the floor. Narrow paths led from one room to another everywhere in the house, making it difficult to even get to the phone.

Dramatic growth continued for five years. We rented more than ten thousand square feet of space in an enormous cinder-block warehouse where our dressing was prepared in two-hundred-gallon tanks and bottles bounced down stainless-steel conveyer belts. A new, fully automatic machine made Jesse's production line obsolete by tirelessly screwing on bottle caps as long as someone kept dumping more caps into its hopper. It was an amazing machine. Inside was a large paddle that constantly rotated caps until, magically, they shot out right-side up and were automatically screwed onto bottles.

Our days when friends and neighbors helped out were long gone. We employed twenty-three full-time workers and had more than fifty commissioned sales reps selling our products nationwide. Replaced by two administrative assistants, an office manager, and two financial people, Carlye had long since left. If this was still a cottage industry, the cottage was very large.

Our recipes had turned into formulas and were produced by people standing on production lines serenaded by the constant noise of large machinery. I was traveling on the road every other week and Mel was immersed in financial statements and production schedules; we hadn't actually cooked anything in months. We longed for the fourteen-hour days in our home kitchen surrounded by family and friends.

Remember

Do

Trust your instincts.

Take chances for the things you care about.

Ask yourself as many questions as it takes to discover where your passion lies.

Don't

Listen to anyone who says your dreams can't come true.

Suppress your passion.

Take the importance of surrounding yourself with the right people lightly.

Your life doesn't have to
fit
neatly between the lines.

Color it any
way you want!

trust it
or adjust it

California Dreaming

Moving On

Cooking in a Bookstore

The great thing about love—whether it's the love of your life or the life you love—is that it's about feelings. The feelings come in many forms and have many names. Whether they're called *instinct* or *intuition*, come from the heart or the gut, feelings are vital to a passionate, meaningful life. You need to completely believe in what you're doing; you need to trust it or adjust it.

Feelings have been—and always will be—the bedrock of our lives. Time and again we've faced potentially life-changing decisions that seemed to offer overwhelming advantages and decided against them. Why? The more logical choices simply didn't *feel* right. Recognizing the value in every experience and checking your dreams for practicality are crucial ingredients for making a life you love, but you must also learn to trust your feelings.

A good life always boils down to proper alignment of the Big 4, and it's important to question what is and isn't working in your life. When you ask yourself if you're still *passionate* about what you're doing, if you're enjoying the *people* you spend time with, and if you love where you *live,* you need to listen carefully to your answers. If the answers aren't an enthusiastic "yes," it's time to make an adjustment. We all need to feel comfortable and to periodically check the Big 4. "Special" deals, "golden" opportunities, and the "easy" way are not special, golden, or easy if they don't feel right. Some people can be successful settling for what others have done or with the usual way of living. It has never worked for us. To live what you love, enthusiasm, instinct, and personal integrity are your best friends.

Behind every setback
is an opportunity.

California Dreaming

Summer 1979

Our cookware store turned out to be a huge success, and we out-grew Peanie's location in the first year. We moved across the street to a larger shopping center and business was booming. But on one of our frequent drives over to Maine for chowder and lobster rolls, we admitted to each other that something was not quite right. We were bored. After three years, the initial challenges of designing the store and learning the business of retailing were long gone. We found ourselves stuck behind a cash register day after day and though we'd worked hard to get there, moving on felt like the right thing to do. We longed for the challenge of creating something from scratch again.

So when someone came along and offered us $150,000, we sold our first business. Trading the '49 Dodge for a VW camper (alas, we did not sell it to Peanie!), we drove across the country with five-year-old Jesse to find the land of milk and honey. We wanted a West Coast version of what we had in Vermont: a house with a pool on a secluded rocky coastline to replace our hilltop home with a view of the mountains. We'd trade New England colonial for Spanish revival, adding a red tile roof and year-round gardens full of tropical flowers and palm trees. We had not even heard of Anguilla, our future home, but were already looking for a tropical paradise . . . just in the wrong place.

Our plan was to open another retail store, this time in a larger market, while ridding ourselves of New England winters at the same time. We were open-minded about where we wanted to live in California and could see advantages to both the northern and southern parts of the state. We loved San Francisco, Palo Alto, and Marin County in the north, but were also drawn to Santa Barbara and La Jolla in the south.

We drove up and down the coast, meeting with real estate brokers and developers searching for our new life. Jesse was too young to realize that his parents were a little left of center, but the real estate people were more suspicious. They failed to see the beauty of living in a VW camper and weren't always sympathetic when we brought our five-year-old to meetings. We're amazed when we think that if cell phones had been prevalent at the time, we might have ended up owning retail stores in California. But in 1979 they weren't, and our contact numbers were usually pay phones in campgrounds.

Still, we loved California, and—being determined—we kept searching. We came close to signing a lease on a fabulous space that included the famous clock tower in San Francisco's Ghirardelli Square, but it was twelve thousand square feet on three floors and we didn't have enough money to buy inventory to fill the space, let alone fixtures and working capital.

We found an ideal location in the Palo Alto Shopping Center but lost out to a local chain of well-established kitchen stores with more experience and money. We were also sure their owners didn't live in a VW camper.

After three months of many false starts and countless rejections, our California dream was beginning to lose its luster and, as September approached, so did the deadline for Jesse's kindergarten registration. We had to settle down somewhere soon.

Just as we were thinking of admitting defeat, we found a space in a new shopping mall in Carlsbad, located between San Diego and Los Angeles. The mall was being built by the May Company and we hit it off with Richard Greene, the man in charge of leasing. Rather than being skeptical of our quirky lifestyle, Richard appeared intrigued. So we found ourselves sitting around a huge conference table, listening carefully as he explained the details of a three-inch-thick document that would be our lease. Jesse sat on the floor playing with his *Star Wars* figures.

"You understand that this is a triple net lease and that you're responsible for building out the space, right?" Richard asked. "That means we'll provide you with a dirt floor and steel studs to separate you from the tenant next door. You'll need to pour a concrete floor, build all the walls, and install a ceiling, plus you're responsible for the electrical, heating, and air-conditioning systems. We also require that you have an architect design your storefront and that it fit in with the overall look of the mall."

"So the landlords don't actually build these malls, do they?" Mel asked. "The tenants pay for everything. Any idea what the average build-out costs?"

"A four-thousand-square-foot store like yours," Richard answered matter-of-factly, "would cost around four hundred thousand dollars. Some tenants sink a lot of money into the storefront; you can spend a hundred thousand on the entrance alone if you let your architect get carried away. I can give you names of two or three guys who've done a lot of work in our malls and are reasonable. If you need bank financing, I'd recommend

Bank of America, which is pretty cooperative. I'll give you a contact name. Any questions?"

"No," I said. "You've been very helpful. We'll study the lease and look for a house to rent."

"A house?" Jesse perked up.

"Yeah, what do you think?" Mel was helping him pack his *Star Wars* collection into its carrying case shaped like Darth Vader's helmet.

"A house sounds good," Jesse said. "How do we find one with a swimming pool?"

"We'll go to a real estate office right now and see what they have for rent."

We thanked Richard Greene, who said to Jesse as he shook his hand, "Good luck with the house search."

Finding a house turned out to be much easier than finding a location for our store. We spent the next three days with rental agents before signing a one-year lease on a brand-new three-bedroom Spanish-style house just like we'd imagined, complete with red tile roof and landscaped yard. Very California. It had no pool but the ocean was only a few blocks away. Its only drawback was the height of the garage door—which clearly hadn't been designed with our VW camper in mind. After just two days a neighbor came over to ask in a frosty voice, "Do you plan on keeping that *truck* parked outside all the time?" Welcome to the suburbs.

We called our movers in Vermont and arranged to get our furniture out of storage and have it delivered to California. In the meantime we slept in sleeping bags on the wall-to-wall carpeting and ate a lot of Chinese takeout. We were still camping—we were just doing it in a house.

Each day we'd go to the mall and watch the construction, marveling at our good fortune in finding such an outstanding location. The section that included our store was a new addition to the mall built to accommodate two new department stores and an additional seventy-five specialty shops. We sat in the existing mall and studied the pedestrian traffic, observing our potential customers. There were fewer people than we'd expected.

Richard Greene had shown us very high sales figures representing a sampling of stores, and we were trying to figure out why some stores seemed to be far busier than others. We noticed that music stores and jewelry shops were especially jammed with customers.

The three of us settled down on a bench near a fountain, Mel and I watching people while Jesse studied a Richard Scarry book. Within minutes I looked at Mel in surprise. "What's going on?" I asked.

"I'm not sure. Doesn't it seem strange that there are so many people here all of a sudden?" Mel asked. "And it's a little odd that almost everyone is wearing a military uniform. I never noticed that before."

"I'm going to ask the guy at the cookie store," I said. "He seems pretty friendly."

I came back with two chocolate chips and an oatmeal raisin. "I learned a lot from the cookie man. First of all, he says we're crazy to think about selling expensive food processors and cookware in this mall. He said we'd be too high-priced for the customers. I showed him the pictures of our old store and he said he thinks we're in the wrong area. Remember when we drove by Camp Pendleton?" I asked.

"Yes," Mel answered. "The broker said it's one of the largest Marine Corps bases in the world."

"Well, apparently this is where they shop," I said.

"Is that a bad thing? It seems like we'd have a captive audience," Mel replied.

I took a deep breath and tried to relay the information I'd just learned. "The people who work on the base get paid every two weeks, and today is payday." The look on Mel's face was halfway between angry and bewildered.

"So?" she asked.

"So, I'm starting to put two and two together. As proud as I am of our country's military, the cookie man told me that the majority of people on the base are single, transient, and not interested in cookware. That's why the music and jewelry stores do so well. The marines are buying gifts for their girlfriends and music to take with them when they're assigned to duty. It makes perfect sense."

"We've made a terrible mistake, haven't we?" Mel asked. "We're going to lose everything if we stay here. If these people don't want to buy what we want to sell, our business will never work. We can't do this." Then the tears came.

"What's wrong, Mom?" Jesse looked up at Mel, and I thought he might start crying, too.

"We haven't signed the lease yet," I reminded her.

"But we did sign the lease on the house," she sobbed. "We'll lose the first and last months' rent—and we just bought a new refrigerator. What if the movers are already on their way?"

"Are we leaving the house?" Jesse asked.

"I think we are," I said. "Let's go. I'll call Richard Greene and tell him what we've decided."

We rode back to the empty house in silence except for a few sniffles from Mel. The neighbor glared when we pulled our VW into the driveway. I thought Mel was going to punch her.

"Where are we going to go?" Jesse asked innocently.

"Maybe California isn't such a great idea right now," I said. "Here's the thing. We love its weather, its architecture, and the idea of a laid-back, beachy sort of lifestyle. But let's face it. Our neighbors have turned out to be anything but laid back and when we pictured ourselves in California, we never imagined that it meant suburbia. It's just not us. I think the only reason we wanted to relocate was because the thought of trying something new was exhilarating. But we'd be crazy to stay here unless we were jumping up and down with enthusiasm. We need to be genuinely happy with our decision. And you know we're not too thrilled about sending Jesse to school here either. Think of this giant school and compare it to the little gem of an elementary school back home. Most people have to spend large sums of money to get their children into a school like ours."

Mel nodded in agreement, and I could see her face brighten with relief. "Why don't you and Jesse start packing up the camper while I call Richard Greene?" I said.

"Hi, Richard," I began. "It's Bob Blanchard."

"How are you coming on the lease?" he asked.

"I'm afraid we've had a change of heart," I said. "We just don't think this market is right for our store. It feels wrong."

"If it's about the cost of the build-out, maybe I can help," he said. "I'll write you a check for ten thousand dollars to help offset the cost."

"That's very nice of you, Richard, but it's not the money. This just doesn't feel like the right place for us. We thought it was, but we made a mistake."

"How about twenty thousand?" he offered.

"Richard, I'm telling you it's not about the money. We're not trying to negotiate a better deal."

"Thirty thousand dollars cash up front!" he said. Clearly he was beginning to worry.

"I'm sorry, Richard. It's just not going to work."

We went out for pizza, and we all started talking at once, flattered that the May Company was offering us so much money just to locate in its mall. But our minds were made up. We planned to begin the drive back to Vermont the next day.

The phone rang at eight o'clock in the morning. "Hi, Bob, it's Richard Greene. I thought I'd see how you were feeling about things this morning. I'm prepared to give you fifty thousand dollars to help you build your store. I think you two would do a beautiful job, and your concept is perfect for our expansion."

"Hold on," I said, covering the receiver. "Mel, he's offering fifty thousand dollars in cash. Are you sure we're not being hasty here?"

"We don't belong here," came her abrupt reply.

"Richard," I said, "I'm going to send the lease back to you. Who knows? Maybe we're passing up the deal of a lifetime, but I don't think so. Thanks so much for everything." I hung up and smiled at Mel and Jesse.

"Let's go home," I said. "If we start driving right now, Jesse will be back in time for his first day of kindergarten."

Moving On
1960-1970

I grew up in New York City alone with my mom. She was a single parent and while life wasn't always easy, it sure was fun. Even as a child, I understood that, financially, we were living on the edge, but somehow we always got by. My mom was determined to give me a well-rounded childhood—no matter what it cost.

She could have chosen to live in a less expensive neighborhood but she was never one to compromise. We lived on Central Park West, went to Broadway shows, and dined at the city's best restaurants. I went to private school and summer camp, took ballet and piano lessons, and learned to ski in Vermont on weekends.

My childhood sounds like one grounded in privilege, but that's only one side of it. My dad was gone, leaving us with no money when I was very young. My mom was strong, beautiful, and artistic, and she had an uncanny ability to convince people that she could do almost anything. She used all these qualities to supplement her meager financial resources, and combined, they magically carried us through life one day at a time. I don't remember ever hearing her say the word *can't*.

My first memories of Mom in the working world were formed by hearing her tell stories of being a model. She was one of those women who made heads turn every time she entered a room, and for ten years she posed for advertising, runway shows, and department stores. I never learned precisely why her modeling career ended, but I remember hearing vague stories about lecherous photographers and creeps who couldn't keep their hands off her.

So she eased herself into another career and soon our apartment was filled with paintings and art supplies. There were easels in every room, some for paper and charcoal drawing, and others for canvas and oils. She'd often paint all day and well into the night; I still remember her—brush in hand, working as she watched Johnny Carson until the wee hours of the morning. To this day I have no idea where she sold all of her artwork, but she found a market somewhere. She produced a prodigious amount of art that was apparently good enough that she sold all of it, earning enough money to pay the rent and my private school tuition.

When I was eight years old my mother decided to spread her wings even farther and, using her artistic talents, became an interior decorator as well as a landlord. I became her willing assistant. It was my first encounter with entrepreneurship. My mother had saved just enough money to rent an unfurnished, unoccupied apartment on East 56th Street, where we spent weekends painting walls and drawing floor plans. I would measure and she would draw.

Once the apartment was painted and my mother's decorating plans completed, we'd hit the auctions. Mom read the paper to see what was coming up for auction that would fit her designs. I'd have fun going along after school and offering my opinion on which piece of furniture I thought would look best in the new apartment. We refinished or repainted furniture when necessary and, in a matter of weeks, listed the apartment in the "For Rent" section of the *New York Times*.

The phone rang off the hook. Within a week we'd found a tenant and rented the apartment with a year's lease. By the time I was twelve, my mother, repeating that same scenario many times over, was managing more than twenty apartments, all of which she'd decorated and subleased at substantial profit.

But times change. A few years later the New York rental market began to falter; Mom's business was slipping away. Overnight, rentals had become a thing of the past; people with money were buying their apartments instead of renting them. Undaunted, Mom entered school and, after six months of classes, proudly announced that she had earned her real-estate license. If she couldn't rent real estate, she was going to sell it. Our days of refinishing furniture and visiting auction houses were over.

Mom started working at an up-and-coming real estate firm on Madison Avenue that was carving out a lucrative niche market by catering to wealthy clients looking for luxury apartments in Manhattan's newly converted co-op buildings. Her first client was Woody Allen; a new career was born, a new adventure begun.

My mom's goals were straightforward: to be a good mother, enjoy a full life by embracing new experiences, and marry a wonderful man with the same objectives. She never did find that perfect man but she scored high in every other regard. Flexibility was an intrinsic part of her nature and helped her overcome setbacks without losing her enthusiasm for her dream.

As for me, she gave me the gift of knowing I can do whatever I want and the courage to follow through. I knew as long as I was doing what I loved, money would follow. And, in general, it has.

Cooking in a Bookstore
April 2003

When our publisher told us we'd be going on a tour for our first book, we momentarily panicked. Actually it was a combination of fear and excitement, not panic. We had no idea what we'd gotten ourselves into and were feeling insecure and a little apprehensive. Our editor explained the details and how an author tour worked, convincing us that we'd be just fine. "You two are always talking to customers of one kind or another," she said. "An author tour is no different."

Of course, we couldn't leave any of this to chance, so we attended several author events at various bookshops in the area to find out just what authors did. It didn't take us long to discover that there was a pattern. Since *A Trip to the Beach* was written as a string of stories, we decided that we'd take turns reading excerpts from the book and answer questions from the audience. We were still nervous when we arrived at our first event but we relaxed more and more with each appearance. Looking back, we can't imagine why we were so scared.

When our publisher told us we'd be going on tour with our second book—*At Blanchard's Table,* a cookbook—real panic set in. We aren't celebrity chefs, nor do we want to be. We love sharing our favorite recipes and encouraging families and friends to cook together, but beyond that we have no interest in touting ourselves as gourmet gurus. How, we wondered, would we hold the attention of an audience that had come to learn about food? Mel could pull off deviled eggs for her seventh-grade class, but this was a different speech altogether!

Leigh Ann, our publicist, called to find out if we had anything specific in mind for the tour. When we said we hadn't thought about it yet, she offered to arrange for someone in each city to make "a little something" ahead of time that we could serve at each bookstore. "That sounds nice," Mel responded absentmindedly. Leigh Ann and I could tell she didn't like the idea at all.

"We need to make the audience feel like they're at the restaurant," Mel said after a thoughtful silence. "You know, take them to Anguilla! If they're going out of their way to come see us, we need to make sure they have a good time. And when people walk into each store, they should smell onions and garlic and spices and whatever it is we're cooking. You can't do that if someone delivers cold food that's prepared ahead of time."

We told Leigh Ann to give us a few days to think and promised to get back to her with a plan. As soon as we hung up I said, "Let's take bags of sand with us and ask everyone to take off their shoes. That would make them feel like they're in Anguilla."

"I don't think so," Mel said, "but keep thinking."

"How about a bamboo thatched roof that we can stand under as we grill food using recipes from the cookbook?"

"That's a great idea," Mel said. "But how do we get it on the plane and fly from Boston to Kansas City to San Francisco?"

"I'll have to design it like a trade show booth. It'll need to fold up so it can be checked as luggage." My mind was already drawing the plans.

"We can grill Jamaican Jerk Chicken and make Banana Cabanas in the blender," she added, "and we'll need a couple of burners for sauces."

We called Leigh Ann and told her our plans for the menu. After a long silence she cautiously responded, "I hate to burst your bubble but you really can't do all that. It's just not practical. As fabulous as it all sounds, you're making this much more complicated than it needs to be. People would be happy if you passed around a plate of cookies. You don't need to serve three courses!"

"Come on, Leigh Ann," Mel said. "You've known us for long enough to know we wouldn't be happy just passing around a plate of cookies. If we're going on a cookbook tour, we're going to cook and it's going to be fun. Otherwise, what's the point?"

"I've organized a lot of cookbook tours and you just don't need to go to all that trouble," she insisted.

"If we can figure out a way to make it work and how to get the food and equipment from city to city, what's the harm in trying? We'll sell more books and everyone will have fun."

"Okay," she conceded. "If you can figure out a way to move that whole operation across the country, promising that you'll be on time for each event, you have my blessing. I know you'll sell lots of cookbooks, which, in the end, is my job. But if it turns out to be too much work, let me know and we'll go back to the cookies."

Mel and I were now more determined than ever to create a fun event at every stop on our tour. This didn't mean we weren't worried about how we were going to pull it off.

"You know, of course," I said cautiously to Mel, "most

bookstores don't have kitchens." I started to picture us hauling huge boxes from airport to airport.

We went to a luggage store and opened every oversized suitcase we could find, comparing the merits and sizes of each. We ended up buying two enormous, black trunks to carry the portable grill, two-burner electric hotplate, blender, food processor, extension cords, and all the forks, knives, spoons, napkins, serving utensils, cutting boards, bowls, dishes, and cups we'd need to serve hundreds of people.

And believe it or not, you can actually find bamboo and thatch on the Internet. A week later Mel had bundles of it delivered to our door in Vermont. I went to work designing a movable thatched hut.

By the time we had gathered all the luggage we'd need for our three-week road trip, along with the two big suitcases holding our portable kitchen, we realized the thatched hut was just a bit over the top. It took us an hour to assemble and another hour to knock down, which was a physical impossibility in many cities, where we'd land at the airport at eleven in the morning needing to be across town and cooking by noon. In the end the bamboo hut bit the dust.

But our determination to create a fun event paid off. Our first stop was the Barnes & Noble bookstore near Lincoln

Center in New York. Leigh Ann had warned us to not get our hopes up for a huge crowd. "New York is a tough market," she'd said. "They're used to big-name authors." It was a gentle way of saying we weren't yet ready for the major leagues.

We grilled spicy chicken, tossed Caesar salad with homemade croutons, and poured Banana Cabanas straight from the blender and, much to our surprise, we had a standing-room-only crowd. The store smelled delicious and the event was a huge success. Word spread quickly to the other bookstores on our tour. Leigh Ann called ahead telling them to get ready. "The Blanchards are coming and they're cooking up a storm."

Nobody knew how much work it took to make these events happen. We'd wash dishes every night in a different hotel room, bake dozens of croutons in a toaster oven at five in the morning, and search high and low for the right ingredients in cities where we'd never been before. In Chicago, we needed Bailey's Irish Cream for the Banana Cabanas, but by the time we arrived all the stores were closed. We called the concierge at our hotel, looking for help. Half an hour later room service delivered thirty miniature bottles of Bailey's arranged on a white tablecloth with thirty tiny glasses. We looked at each other and laughed hysterically, realizing they thought we were throwing some kind of wacky party. And we were—just not right then or right there.

Remember

Do

Experience all that life has to offer.

Believe in yourself. That's when the magic begins.

Prioritize all aspects of your life in order to
clarify your goals.

Don't

Worry about things you can't control.

Allow other people to make your choices.

Be afraid to share your dreams with friends and family.

Live with your eyes
wide open,

so you don't miss a thing.

if you want it,
make it

Best of Both Worlds

Back to School

One way or another, life is a rush. It can be a rush of time flying by us, or it can be a rush of excitement sweeping us up. Time flies on its own. The rush of excitement comes through the actions of people building a life that they love. You have to create it yourself.

From the clarifying birth of Jesse that encouraged us to step back from the little threads to see the big patterns, we've used the events of our lives to forge a life we love. Each day we look for dreams that will provide meaning and significance. Then we develop the tools and skills by applying the Big 4—passion, people, location, and money—to evaluate where we are going. Above all, we trust our feelings about the decisions and the choices that we need to make to bring the dream to life.

The real rush begins with action. Dreams are wonderful. However, doing something each and every day to put our decisions and choices into action is what we love. Building and living a passionate life requires focus and attention. We like the action. We seek the action. Action—building a house in Vermont, arranging new working relationships in a restaurant, or earning an education in a totally new area of expertise—means a commitment to a fresh project, the latest dream, and our newest love.

Each day—each new day and each today—is a time to accomplish something. Big or small, each day's action builds the rush that comes from a life of excitement. We make it happen. We act. That is how we live a life we love.

Enjoy life's detours.
They often provide
some of life's greatest
memories.

Best of Both Worlds

Summer 1998

It was the middle of July, and Mel and I were counting down the days until we closed the restaurant for hurricane season. We sat on our balcony, watching the waves gently breaking on the shore of Long Bay.

"Do you think we should close a little earlier?" I asked.

"No," Mel said. "The staff is counting on the income through August. It wouldn't be fair. Besides, we've already told the hotels when we're closing and we have a few August reservations."

"I know, but it's hard to wait until September." I felt guilty for wanting to close early but as business slows in summer, the days seem to drag and I long for more stimulation. "I miss

Vermont," I blurted out, "not in the winter, but I can almost smell the fresh-cut hay in the summer. And I miss the way it stays light until nine o'clock at night."

We sat in silence, lost in our memory of New England summers. "Are you sick of Anguilla?" Mel finally asked.

"No. I love it here!" I answered. "Sometimes I just miss Vermont. I wish we had a place to go up there when we close for the season. I feel like such a gypsy spending two months visiting friends and staying in hotels." The old vagabond days of taking a VW van across the country and all around California were not nearly as appealing now.

My comment, which was intended as a bit of humor, struck a nerve in Mel. She shot me a look of disdain.

"Do you remember how badly we wanted to move to Anguilla?" she began. "Look at what we have here. Look where we live. Do you see that beautiful water out there right in front of our balcony? Do you appreciate that we have a great staff at the restaurant? Don't you realize what a great life we have? Don't get me wrong. I miss Vermont, too, but I could never give this up."

I felt like an ingrate—a spoiled little boy who didn't appreciate the birthday present his doting parents had just given him. Just then a green-and-white sailboat glided past our house. I thought about swimming out to it, climbing aboard, and disappearing, shamefully, over the blue horizon. What was wrong with me, anyway? Saying I missed Vermont was like being unfaithful to Anguilla. I should be thrown off the island, but not before being publicly humiliated and offered up as an example of the kind of foreigner who should never be allowed to live here.

"Listen," Mel said. "I have an idea." I swallowed hard and readied myself for what was next. Mel always has ideas, and sometimes they scare the living daylights out of me. "Why don't we look around in Vermont when we go back in September and see if we can find a piece of land we can afford to buy? Maybe in a few years we can build a little house so we have a place to go during the off-season. It doesn't have to be an all-or-nothing kind of thing. We could run the restaurant and still enjoy Vermont for part of the year."

"You're a genius." This time Mel's idea was perfect; I was feeling better already. "It would also give Jesse a place to go," I added. "Maybe we could build a little studio where he could pursue his painting."

"Let's not get too carried away," Mel said. "First we have to find a piece of land that we like and can afford. That might not be so easy."

We spent the rest of July and all of August dreaming about Vermont's rolling hills, longing for land with lots of privacy and a beautiful view. We studied a state map and considered each town and what it had to offer.

As we were researching our new town, our thoughts kept coming back to our old hometown of Norwich simply because it felt like an old friend and we missed the friends we'd left behind when we'd moved to Anguilla. There was Dan & Whit's, the wonderful rambling general store. Its aisles are filled with groceries, wine, clothing, hardware, grain, gardening supplies, woodstoves, plumbing supplies, paint, all captivatingly irresistible. There's Dartmouth College just a mile away, offering an outstanding cultural life that kept us stimulated and feeling less isolated—and created an emotional tie back to the Dartmouth medical center that had saved Jesse's life and put ours on a totally different course. Then there's the handful of great restaurants—many of which are family-run—all just minutes away. And we could live on a dirt road with no noise and no traffic. How could we consider anywhere but Norwich?

Happily, we found the property of our dreams on a perfect Vermont September day. The leaves were just beginning to turn, and a patchwork of yellow, red, and orange covered the hills as far as the eye could see. The air was cool, clear, and crisp and smelled unmistakably of fall.

Mel and I stood with Susan Green, our friend and broker, looking out at the view, and we felt like we were on top of the world. Susan pointed out the landmarks. "That's Moose Mountain straight ahead, and Smarts Mountain is over there; there's Cube, and Moosilauke to the north. Look south, there's Hanover, there's Whaleback ski area, and over there is Mount Kearsarge. See it? It's way off in the distance."

"What do you think?" I asked Mel, knowing the answer before she said a word.

"Do you think the owner would consider any financing?" she asked.

"We can ask," Susan said. "Let's put in an offer and see what he says." This time around a broker named Green and the hunt for a new property all added up, the way it never had with Richard Greene in California. It felt right and we knew it would happen.

By the time we flew back to Anguilla in November, we had become, once again, Vermonters. As much as we love Anguilla— and we love it more than we can put into words—it felt great to own land back home. Although we had no immediate plans to start building, I returned to the island armed with enough books on home construction and design to outfit a small architectural firm. I intended to spend my spare time drawing plans for our ideal Vermont home during the winter.

Jesse, having finished college and now an art teacher in New York, came to visit. As soon as he heard about our land, he realized that he too was being called by his Vermont roots and asked if we'd let him put up a cabin where he could live and paint.

"Of course you can," I said. "I get more and more excited about building a house as I draw the plans. Do you have any interest in building it with Mom and me this summer? We could build a barn, which could be your studio, and you could live in the house this winter as soon as we get it insulated. It may not be finished but it will at least be warm."

"I'd love to help you build a house!" Jesse said. "Could we really do it in a summer? When would we start? Do we have enough money? Are you sure we could do it?" Mel and I had asked ourselves all the same questions and weren't 100 percent sure of our answers. Still, we felt that if we wanted it to happen, things would fall into place; or so we hoped.

Once Jesse was on board, Mel and I sprang into action. I'd dreamed about the three of us building a house together but, believing it was just a romantic notion, never thought we'd really do it. Timing is everything in life, and this seemed perfect.

Getting a mortgage turned out to be a little tricky since our income came from the Caribbean. Mel started making inquiries, and soon we were filling out application forms. "I'm not sure if this is going to work," she said. "They don't seem to know what to do with us. As usual, our life doesn't fit into those little boxes on their forms. As soon as they see our address, red flags go up. Even more confusing, our tax returns show exemptions for living in a foreign country. We're going to have to find a banker who trusts us and is willing to take a little bit of risk. Keep your fingers crossed."

I hate banks and worrying about money even more, so I left it in Mel's capable hands. Meanwhile my building plans were becoming more and more elaborate and I was having the time of my life. One way or another we were going to build this house, or so I said aloud. Secretly, I felt it was too good to be true—but I kept on drawing.

Next to money, our beloved restaurant was, oddly, our biggest obstacle. Who would keep it running if we spent time in Vermont? Neither of us had missed a single night of work since opening; it was a daunting prospect. My presence on the floor, and Mel's in the kitchen, were integral parts of the Blanchard's experience. I seated every customer and opened every bottle of wine, while Mel cooked and arranged every plate of food that left the kitchen. We did the prep work together during the day, assuming our respective places each night. It didn't seem possible to replace us, and we weren't about to close for six months. We couldn't ask that of our staff—nor could we afford it.

As we were thinking about how to rearrange our lives, an amazing thing happened. One of our customers offered us an astonishing sum of money to buy the restaurant. We talked nonstop about selling, and the thought of having enough cash to build our house with enough left over for a savings account was compelling.

We loved the challenge of starting a business from scratch and getting it up and running. Once the kinks were worked out and the systems in place, we tended to get bored, and selling had always been the next step. We'd done it many times before and it appeared that we were destined to repeat the pattern. The money was just too much to pass up.

"But what about our staff?" Mel asked as we continued to weigh the pros and cons of selling. "Think about Lowell, Miguel, and Clinton. And what about Bug? And Garrilin and Ozzie and Hughes? And everyone else, for that matter. How could we just leave them? Do you really want to do that?"

My heart sank and rebounded all at once. Mel was right. There was no way we could leave our staff, even if it meant having more money than we'd ever thought possible. This business was different. Anguilla was different. It wasn't about money. Our staff had become family, and we simply couldn't imagine turning our backs on them. What if we sold the restaurant and they didn't get along with the new owners? Worse yet, what if the new owners didn't like them? No. This just wasn't going to happen. We couldn't do it. There had to be a way we could spend more time in Vermont and still keep the restaurant.

We turned down the cash offer with one phone call and that was that. Our dream of a large bank balance disappeared into thin air.

We met with our staff the next afternoon and, opening our hearts, explained everything. They listened quietly as we told them how much we loved them but how homesick we were. We outlined the few solutions we'd come up with, none of which was simple, and asked what they thought about our plans. We needed to know how they felt.

They were silent. We felt as if we'd betrayed all of them by simply bringing up the subject of returning to Vermont—even for part of the year. *But no,* I wanted to shout, *don't you understand? We want to work with you forever. We love you! We just need to figure out a way to get back to Vermont when Anguilla slows down in the low season. Please don't be angry.*

Garrilin was the first to speak. "I understand about being homesick. My family is far away and I miss them, too. We can do it, man. We can run this place without you."

A few others nodded hesitantly in agreement and then there was more silence. "Okay," Mel said confidently. "If you're willing to give it a try, we believe you can do it. We've come up with a plan we feel might work. Clinton, how would you feel about taking over as chef when I'm not here? I know you have it in you and I can teach you everything you need to know." More silence. Clinton was our rock. He was honest, reliable, and loved learning new things. He'd come to Blanchard's after years of working construction and quickly made himself at home in the kitchen.

"Lowell," I said, "we'd like to teach you to take my place. Actually, you would be a little bit of me and a little bit of Mel. You'd do the prep work with Clinton in the mornings, run the dining room floor at night, and you and Mel would do the bookkeeping together long distance." Lowell nodded and gave us a look that said he was up for giving it a try. "And Miguel, how would you like to be the wine steward? You seem to have the interest and I'll teach you everything I know. Plus, we'd like you to be the assistant manager and help Lowell oversee the whole show."

"Yah mon," Miguel said, peering over his shades. "I'd love to learn more about the wine. That cool with me."

Mel went on to explain our vision and how it could be implemented. "Ozzie, you, Hughes, and Garrilin will help Clinton; Alwyn and everyone else would work the floor, backing up Lowell and Miguel. I really believe this can work."

From that day forward life at Blanchard's took on new meaning. A closeness developed among us that none of us could have predicted. We spent three months teaching and training while they soaked up as much knowledge as possible. Lowell and Mel created a daily report form that Lowell would fax to Vermont, keeping us in constant contact. Miguel and I tasted wine after wine until we were both confident that he knew most of the bottles in our cellar.

I can still remember the first night Mel stepped back and allowed Clinton to take the place of honor at the stove. Mel watched his hand shake uncontrollably as he spooned couscous onto a plate. He was scared to death and Mel had a hard time holding back tears. She later told me that she'd felt a huge pang of guilt for putting a mellow guy like Clinton in such a high pressure position. It hadn't occurred to her that Clinton was probably as grateful as he was scared to have the opportunity to take her place.

By the time spring came around, our staff was eager to show us—and our customers—that they could run the restaurant without us. Meanwhile I'd created a set of blueprints for our future home in Vermont and felt as if I'd studied enough books to earn a degree in architecture. Mel had, thankfully, secured a mortgage.

Some of the staff came to the airport to wish us luck. They also felt they needed to constantly assure us that we had nothing to worry about. But we knew the restaurant was in their hands and that they would make us proud. "We can do it!" were the last words I remember them yelling as we walked out onto the runway.

We broke ground on our Vermont house the first of May, knowing we had to get back to Anguilla by the time the season kicked off again in the fall. The house needed to be heated so Jesse could move in and we could go back to work. Our November deadline was very real.

The immensity of the project dawned on me the first day we started work. I'd made a materials list for every stage of construction, and the first delivery had just arrived. Jesse and Mel stood by ready, waiting for my instructions. My crew—as it were—had lots of enthusiasm but little experience. I'd grown up designing and building everything from furniture to houses, so I was confident that I could show them what to do. But for three of us to build a fourteen-hundred-square-foot art studio and a five-thousand square-foot house in such a short period of time was more challenging than I'd realized.

By the third week of May we were on a roll. "Fifteen feet, ten inches," Jesse called out to Mel. I was up on the staging near the ridge of the studio, holding one end of the tape measure with Jesse on the deck of the second floor holding the other. Mel cut the rafters and handed them to Jesse, who then helped me nail them into place.

"My fingers are killing me," Jesse said as we put our tools away. I showed him my blisters to assure him that he was not the only one who needed to get into shape. "Comes with the job," I said. "They'll turn into calluses soon enough and by then you won't feel a thing." I could tell Jesse was having second thoughts about the whole project as he nursed his wounds that night.

By July, Jesse could swing a hammer as well as he could wield a paintbrush. He took great pride in being able to sink a sixteen-penny nail with only three blows like his dad. Mel became the official operator of the slide compound saw and mastered the art of cutting all the framing materials to the exact measurements as Jesse and I called them out. In between cuts she'd phone the gang at the restaurant to hear how things were going. The staff delighted in telling Mel all the news.

"Mel, listen to this one," Lowell would say, continuing with a story about a customer or a delivery or a leak in the roof. They shared every detail and always had more questions about situations none of us had predicted.

One day Lowell passed the phone to Clinton. "Hey, Mel, Clinton here. We had a little problem last night. A man send his tuna back in the kitchen. He say it overcook."

"Was it overcooked?" Mel asked.

"Yeah. But we made him a next one."

"Was he happy then?"

"Well, not really. He send it back again."

"What happened?" Mel asked.

"Mel, I think the man jus' don' like tuna," Clinton said as honestly as he could.

"So what did you do the second time around?"

"He order lobster instead."

"Was he happy then?" Mel asked.

"Yeah. Lowell say the man really happy when he leff."

"Is there anything else you want to tell me?" Mel asked, sensing there was more to the story.

"Well, not really. But Lowell wants to talk to you again."

"Hey, Mel, it's Lowell. I hope you're not angry but . . . " He paused.

"What's the matter, Lowell?"

"We didn't charge the man for his dinner." Mel could tell from his voice that Lowell was worried he'd overstepped his bounds. How could he give away money that wasn't his?

"Lowell, I'm speechless. You are absolutely amazing," Mel said.

"I'm sorry. I guess I shouldn't have done that," Lowell replied, clearly regretting his decision.

"You did exactly the right thing," Mel assured him. "You've really come a long way. The fact that you understand that making customers happy is our ultimate goal is a huge accomplishment. A year ago you would have been shocked if Bob didn't charge someone to apologize for a problem. Now look at you. I wish I was there to give you a hug."

"Man, I glad you said that. I was pretty sure I did the right thing but somehow, I was scared I make a mistake. Business this time of year is pretty slow and I know we need all the money we can get."

"Lowell, we trust you to make the right decisions and wouldn't have left the restaurant in your hands if we felt otherwise. You're terrific."

"Thanks," was all he said.

Lowell and Mel talked every day and worked through the

glitches as they came along. Mel loved building the house but was thrilled to have the restaurant still part of her daily routine. She found the combination invigorating.

The three of us worked seven days a week, twelve to fourteen hours a day, and had the time of our lives. Our friend—and skilled carpenter—Donny French stopped by as often as he could to lend us a hand. His expertise was more than welcome. During the course of the summer other friends and neighbors helped out on weekends or after work, which made it even more fun. With our deadline growing near, we needed all the help we could get. Our budget wouldn't allow us to hire professionals, but that wasn't why so many people were helping. It was a memorable experience for everyone.

Mel and I were nearly six thousand miles away in Anguilla while Jesse was in college, and the distance often seemed agonizingly vast. Reuniting for this project was a dream come true.

A light snow fell in early October and we were running out of time. Although we'd planned to do everything ourselves except plumbing and electrical work, we ended up hiring out the insulation and Sheetrocking as well. They're nasty jobs and we would never have finished in time.

We moved back to Anguilla in time for Thanksgiving, and Jesse moved into the house—roughly finished as it was. The kitchen appliances were in and his bathroom upstairs was functional if not beautiful. But it was the studio that changed his life. Jesse began his full-time career as an artist, and to this day he paints for a living. He's since married and moved away from home, but his studio and the memories of that summer will remain his forever.

We worried a little about fitting back into the restaurant's routine, since the staff had settled into a new rhythm with new responsibilities. It was clear after the first night that everything and nothing had changed.

"Bob," said Miguel. "Taste this wine and tell me what you think of it."

Lowell chimed in a few minutes later, "Bob, would you take an order from the people on table two?"

In the kitchen Ozzie said, "Mel, you still want me to help Clinton or are you moving back in now?"

"Let's see if we can do it together," Mel said. And we did. And we do so to this day.

Back to School

July 1984

"But there must be some guidelines," Mel argued into the phone. "Yes, we've already spoken with the County Extension Service and the Vermont Department of Health. Look." She rolled her eyes at me, a look that meant she was talking to either a bureaucrat or a buffoon or possibly both. "We're just trying to get some information on bottling food safely and thought you'd be able to help."

Melinda listened for the man on the other end of the line to explain before continuing. "Uh-huh. Uh-huh. Well, thanks for your time. Bye." She slammed the phone down in frustration.

"Sounded like he wasn't very helpful," I said.

"Very helpful? Ha! Listen to this." Mel was disgusted. "The FDA is, and I quote, 'The FDA is a corrective agency, not a preventive agency.' What that means is that they wait for someone to get sick before they come shut you down. They have absolutely no interest in helping us figure out how to do this."

"There must be someone who can help," I said. "We're not the first people in the world to bottle salad dressing and fudge sauce."

"It's time to get Jesse from school," Mel said. "Let's talk more in the car."

Jesse was busy playing in the schoolyard and didn't see us drive up so we parked and sat to watch. He was kicking around a red rubber ball with his friends Peter and Patrick. He finally spotted us, picked up his backpack, and came running over, talking as he climbed into the backseat. "Are we testing more products today? 'Cause Peter and Patrick would like to help."

"I think we're done testing for a few days," Mel answered. "We're having trouble figuring out how to prevent our dressings and sauces from spoiling once they're bottled and shipped to the stores. It's kind of like science."

"I wish I'd paid more attention in chemistry class," I added.

"Maybe you should go to the library," Jesse offered. "That's what Mrs. Falk always tells us to do when we need information."

"That's a great idea," Mel said. "Let's go to the Dartmouth library and look for books on food production. Do you have homework you can work on while we're doing ours?"

The three of us spent the rest of the afternoon at Dartmouth, settling in at a long oak table whose surface was soon covered by books and papers. Jesse did his third-grade math homework while Mel and I frantically researched food safety information.

We left the library recharged and loaded with facts. Food toxicology, as we found it was called, was the area we needed to focus on. We also found out that the University of Massachusetts at Amherst had a food toxicology department. We wrote down the name of its director.

We absorbed a lot of information about producing shelf-stable products over the next few months, including the fact that adding preservatives to any recipe was the easiest way to prevent spoilage in packaged foods. We telephoned UMass which led us to Dr. Spiegel, a food consultant in Boston. "Just a little sodium benzoate and all bacteriological growth is halted," he explained.

Since we were committed to making all-natural products, that wasn't for us.

In order for our company to succeed, we needed to do more than chemistry homework; we also had to research our competition. In between meetings with Dr. Spiegel, designing labels, and testing products, Mel, Jesse, and I took weekend trips to New York. We loved being able to leave our quiet Vermont hilltop in the morning and arrive in New York in time for lunch.

With no time to squander, our trips were brief. We studied the packaging on every bottle of dressing and sauce we could find at Zabar's, Balducci's, Macy's, and The Food Emporium. Jesse was the first to notice that many of their labels were red, so we looked carefully at each label for color and design ideas to help our products stand out from the crowd.

A friend's father suggested that we hire a market research company to analyze the competition and identify ways to best market our product. But we thought marketing was one of the most interesting and personal parts of the job and couldn't imagine turning it over to someone else; besides, we couldn't afford their fee. We also loved having an excuse to go to New York and always managed to find time for a meal at Jesse's favorite Japanese restaurant.

By the end of the day we'd have the car loaded with shopping bags filled with samples of all the competition. Once we arrived back home in Vermont we'd carry everything inside, spread the samples out on the dining room table, and study each detail closely. We made lists of ingredients, the number of ounces in each jar, and how much each sold for at every store.

Dr. Spiegel taught us the proper pH levels for salad dressing and how to prevent mold from forming by using high temperatures to pack dessert sauces. He recommended a food lab in Boston that would analyze each of our products and use the results to create a batch-by-batch testing procedure.

"You need to establish exact systems for manufacture," he explained. "To maintain quality control, each batch must be prepared precisely the same way. And you'll need to set acceptable limits of bacteria and appropriate levels of mold and yeast spores."

While the chemistry was necessary, and we carefully followed all of Dr. Spiegel's advice, frankly, we weren't terribly interested. Meanwhile business was booming.

We had gone from kitchen blenders to 150-gallon stainless-steel tanks in a few short months and we still couldn't keep up with orders. An Oriental salad dressing with toasted sesame seeds was one of our best-selling products. We'd gone from one-pound jars of sesame seeds to twenty-five-pound cartons; from twenty-five-pound cartons to fifty-five-gallon drums; and from fifty-five-gallon drums to entire pallets of fifty-five-gallon drums. There was just no way our home oven could keep up with demand.

A distributor that supplied Korean markets in New York was one of our biggest accounts, and it was going through our Sesame Seed Dressing by the truckload. Orders from smaller accounts were quickly piling up as we struggled to supply our largest customers. We were toasting fifty pounds of sesame seeds at a time and it wasn't enough.

I woke Mel excitedly early one morning with a terrific idea. "What if we ask Bernie at the bagel place to toast the seeds in his giant oven? It could be the perfect solution."

A few hours later we had more than a thousand pounds of sesame seeds evenly toasted a magnificent golden brown. "Perfect," I said as we loaded tubs of toasted seeds into our truck. We mixed batch after batch of Sesame Seed Dressing and soon had all of our backorders filled. I was quite pleased with my brainstorm.

Two months later at the Fancy Food Show, Mel and I were talking to the Macy's Cellar buyer when, suddenly, *pow!* a bottle of our dressing exploded on the shelf behind us, followed by someone across the aisle shouting something about a fireworks display in the Blanchard & Blanchard booth. We watched as several more caps blew off their bottles.

"Wow! That dressing really packs a punch," the Macy's buyer said with a grin. A food buyer for many years, she found it amusing; Mel and I were mortified. Excusing myself to clean up the mess, I anxiously called Dr. Spiegel in Boston to find out what was happening.

We had our answer within an hour. After asking me dozens of questions, Dr. Spiegel told me what went wrong. "You'll have to recall the bottles shipped from the batches of dressing made using the seeds you toasted at the bagel place. You only have to worry about people getting hit by flying bottle caps; the dressing itself isn't harmful. Remember when I told you every single batch had to be prepared exactly the same way?"

"Yes," I answered quietly.

"Think about what's used to make bagels."

My mind was a blur. I could barely wait to call the office to find out how many bottles needed to be recalled, let alone take any time to think about ancient history.

"Yeast!" he shouted into the phone. "That's the enemy. There was enough yeast in the air from bagels to contaminate your sesame seeds. As the yeast grew, it created enough pressure to pop off the caps. It's like bread rising."

He could tell I was not taking this well.

"Don't worry," he said reassuringly. "If this is your worst problem, you'll be in excellent shape. Welcome to the world of packaged foods."

Remember

Do

Take one step at a time and you'll get it done.

Learn that a certain amount of calculated risk can be energizing and have a positive effect on your life.

Don't

Stay in a job you don't enjoy.

Hesitate to share your enthusiasm.

Underestimate the power of spending time with enthusiastic people.

To live a life you love means more than just putting in time, earning money, and coexisting with others.

It means to live a life of
passion,
significance,
and
meaning.

living
(in a material world)

We Love It When the Good Guy Wins

Second Family

Our dreams are real dreams. They are more than rags-to-riches fairy tales; they are more than a fantasy of living in an island paradise; they are more than book signings, television shows, and product lines. We love our life. Our life means more to us than paying the bills, meeting our obligations, and buying us time.

We live a life that acknowledges the significance of every experience we have. While we deal with the practicalities of location, money, people, and passion, we trust our feelings and ourselves. We love what we do. That love removes the risks, drives us, and gets us up hills and through rough spots. Having a life we love moves us into the rush of excitement that comes with action and commitment.

To live a life you love is more than just putting in time, earning money, and coexisting with people. It is to live a life with passion, significance, and meaning. We believe in good guys; we believe in each other, family, and second families. Together we value dreams, decisions, and action. Our life is a series of positive acts with purpose.

Life is to be lived and to be loved. It is more than accepting the expectation for the common life. Together we insist on living our dreams and thereby loving our life. If you truly live what you love, you are rebelling against the common life. You are choosing the unusual over the usual! We find those who support dreams, and we join with them in bringing fulfillment to us all. *Vive la révolution!*

Wouldn't it be awful to live your
whole life and then say
"Wait!
I need another chance.
I just wanted to try this
one thing."

We Love It When the Good Guy Wins

March 1987

Commerce occurs when someone has something to sell that someone else wants to buy. A simple thing, we thought, when we were starting our salad dressing company on a shoestring budget. One of our biggest challenges was locating a supplier for bottles.

We needed twenty cases of empty bottles so we could fill them with salad dressing and introduce our line at the Gourmet Products Show. Mel drove our station wagon to Boston with enough cash to buy the bottles. Her first stop was a company called Glass Unlimited. Its full-page ad in the yellow pages promised the largest selection of bottles at the lowest prices. Mel met with a salesman who adamantly refused to split any pallet—and each pallet held more than a hundred cases of bottles. Even one pallet was way out of our price range; we just needed a few cases. Besides, a pallet would never fit into our station wagon.

With the yellow pages sitting on the seat next to her, Mel worked her way through every bottle supplier in the Boston area, eventually finding herself, tense after driving through a rough neighborhood, at an ancient warehouse in Everett, just over the Tobin Bridge. Israel Andler & Sons had been selling bottles in Boston for generations, and Murray Andler met with Mel, walking her through the old brick warehouse where he personally cut open a shrink-wrapped pallet of bottles.

"Buy as many or as few as you want, my dear," he said. "You can drive your car through that door and we'll load it up for you."

By the time Mel left, she'd eaten rugelach and admired family photos with the entire Andler family. They waved goodbye, wishing her luck.

That was at the beginning of Blanchard & Blanchard, and soon our business was growing by leaps and bounds. Of course, our demand for bottles skyrocketed as well; in about four years we were buying tractor-trailer loads of glass bottles from Murray

Andler and had become a thirty-thousand-dollar-per-month customer—a respectable account.

One day I got a call from a salesman at Glass Unlimited in Boston asking for an appointment to show us his line of bottles. I told him we were pretty busy, but he was insistent and I finally gave in, scheduling a meeting with him the next day.

Mel and I were watching from my office window as the Glass Unlimited salesman struggled up the steps carrying his briefcase along with several cases of bottles. He passed through our loading area just as the crew was unloading a forty-four-foot tractor-trailer filled with a new shipment of bottles from Andler—all on pallets.

"That's the same guy," Mel whispered, "the same one who wouldn't sell to me the first time I went to Boston."

I wanted to make him wait a little while but Mel reminded me that we were above that sort of behavior and went out to greet him. She brought the salesman into our office, where he promptly dumped the cases of bottles on a table. He gave each of us his best salesman's handshake and began his dog-and-pony show.

"I can save you a pile of money on your salad dressing bottles," he said confidently.

"That's not possible," I replied.

"Look." He ignored me. "I know you're buying your glass from Andler and I know how much you're using. Based on your volume, I can sell you glass for much less."

"Do you remember my wife, Melinda?" I asked.

"I'm sorry, but I can't say that I do." He was clearly not expecting my question.

"She tried to buy a few cases from you when we first started out and, apparently, it wasn't worth your while to split a pallet. Murray Andler, on the other hand, brought her to his warehouse, opened several pallets, and told her she could buy as many bottles as she needed. He loaded them into our car himself."

Undaunted, he answered, "Glass Unlimited is a big company and we sell more glass than anyone in New England."

"Let me get this right," Mel replied. "The Andler family helped us get our company going, has always delivered on time, and gave us credit when we were going through difficult times. Now that we're spending thirty thousand dollars a month, you want to undercut them. Did I get that right?"

"May I just give you some pricing?" Glass-man was really off his stride now.

"That isn't necessary," Mel said. "We aren't interested."

"I'll just leave a price list and my card, in case you change your mind." He closed his briefcase and stood up.

"Would you do me just one favor?" Mel asked.

"Sure," he beamed, thinking he might be getting somewhere after all.

"The next time a struggling new company wants to buy a few cases of glass, please think twice before turning them away."

Second Family

January 2004

The Northeast was in the middle of a deep freeze, with temperatures well below zero, and several customers at the restaurant tried to get us to reschedule our trip. We were leaving the next morning—along with our whole staff—for a visit to Vermont. None of them had ever seen snow or experienced temperatures much below seventy degrees. Customers implied that we were acting irresponsibly by exposing our trusting staff to such dangerously severe weather. We had already wondered the same thing.

I was at a table helping a couple choose a wine when Lowell whispered in my ear, "Ozzie needs to see you in the kitchen." Usually I'm summoned to the kitchen when the gas runs out or the water pump stops working or some other mechanical problem arises. I excused myself from the table and rushed back to see what was going on.

As soon as I rounded the corner, I could tell a heated discussion was in progress. "Bob, Bob, come settle the score. Come now."

Mel and I were always asked to mediate. Heaven knows why they think we can answer questions like "Which goes faster, a cruise ship or a speedboat?"

Ozzie persisted. "Come, Bob. You gotta say what it 'tis. You gotta help us here."

The entire staff had taken sides in the debate. Tarah said she'd heard on CNN that it was so cold up north your eyeballs could freeze. And Bug was trying to convince everyone that it was too cold for cars to start and we wouldn't be able to go anywhere.

"I don't believe that true, Bob. Tell 'em," Ozzie begged.

It took only a minute for me to convince them that there was nothing to worry about. The debate was just their way of expressing their excitement about the trip.

"Bob, what should we wear on the plane?" Garrilin asked. "Will it be cold as soon as we get off?"

"The most important thing is to dress conservatively," I said, looking at Rinso. "No Bob Marley T-shirts and no dark shades."

"Yeah man," Miguel added. "U.S. Immigration don' make no joke. It ain' like goin' St. Martin."

"I don' even walk with my passport when I go St. Martin," Ozzie said. "Immigration know me, man."

"U.S. Immigration is definitely not like St. Martin," I added. "If you look like you might cause any trouble whatsoever, they'll pull you aside and couldn't care less if you miss your flight while they check you out."

"Just wear a clean, long-sleeved shirt and a nice pair of pants," Mel said. "We have a friend meeting us at the airport in Boston with boxes of warm clothes for everyone."

"U.S. Immigration is serious business," Lowell added, just to make sure everyone understood.

By the end of the night everyone was still nervous about what to expect but ready to give it a try. Hughes and Ozzie announced that they were planning to stay up all night. They were going to a reggae concert after work and didn't see the point of sleeping for just a few hours. "We gonna sleep at the airport. You just wake us when you get there."

Even at five-thirty in the morning the air was hot and steamy. It took only seconds to scan the small, open-air Anguilla terminal and determine that none of our staff was there. If Hughes and

Ozzie were sleeping, we sure couldn't find them. Our flight was scheduled to depart at 7:00 a.m. and we waited quietly in disbelief.

"Maybe they chickened out," Mel said.

"Maybe they really did believe their eyeballs would freeze," I added.

You'd think that after so many years of living in Anguilla, we'd understand the true meaning of "Island Time."

At 6:15 Ozzie and Hughes arrived, dressed for travel and ready to go. They handed Mel their passports, correctly assuming that she'd take care of all the formalities. Gradually everyone else trickled in; by 6:30 we headed through security.

Everyone waved good-bye to their family and friends, many of whom had come to see them off. As the American Eagle plane rose up high over Anguilla, we all pointed out familiar landmarks on the distant ground below.

"Look," Clinton said. "See Blanchard's there." Everyone on the left side of the plane craned their necks to see the restaurant, now just a tiny speck on the beach.

Ozzie's nose pressed against the window in amazement. "Nothin' out there but water," he said almost to himself.

The approach into San Juan takes you over craggy mountains that eventually give way to concrete, high-rises, and traffic jams. As the landing gear was lowered, Tarah looked out the window in awe and said, "This place don' have any room to breathe. Look how many houses they have so close together." San Juan was no longer the paradise she'd imagined.

We boarded the airplane to Boston with everyone relatively subdued. Lunch was served and we settled in for the movie.

"Watch it, Nemo," Clinton shouted. "Don't go in there, Nemo." Clinton was engrossed with the adventures of that little fish, and it was immediately clear that he was going to enjoy every bit of this trip. He immersed himself in every tiny experience along the way.

"Hold 'er, Cap," Hughes called out as we banked sharply to line up with the runway for landing. "Hold 'er, now." I saw the flight attendants watching Hughes, who was thoroughly enjoying the ride.

"Look," Lowell said. "Snow on the ground. Look at the white." It was snowing lightly as we landed, which is just what we'd hoped for. As we waited for our luggage, our ten travelers—who had been nervous about frozen eyeballs and broken engines the night before—were all outside the terminal scraping up what little snow was on the ground and enjoying their first snowball fight. We passed out jackets, hats, and gloves and attracted more than a little attention at Logan Airport.

As we approached our house in Vermont, they began to see

what real snow looked like. We put the two rented Ford Expeditions into four-wheel drive and slowly climbed up our hill, surrounded on each side by six-foot snowbanks.

No one rushed to open the car doors once we'd arrived and we wondered if they'd already had enough. Now that they'd seen snow, maybe they felt it was time to go back to Anguilla.

Finally Mel and I encouraged everyone to get out of the cars and meet our friend Donny. He'd built a huge bonfire behind the barn, thinking it would keep everyone warm, at least for a while. Before we knew it everyone was outside throwing snowballs and watching the flames light up the crisp, crystal-clear northern night sky. Mel taught Garrilin how to lie on her back and make an angel in the snow; she didn't want to stop.

"I love Vermont!" Garrilin screamed at the top of her lungs.

"I'd come back here anytime," Hughes added. "This is cool. This really cool."

We had a busy schedule trying to cram as much as possible into our short visit. The first morning we cooked a hearty breakfast with eggs, bacon, sausage, pancakes, and Vermont maple syrup. As we were finishing breakfast, Alfonso called from Anguilla. He wasn't able to join us and was heartbroken about not coming. We left him with a key to the restaurant so he could check on it while we were away.

"Hey, Alfonso," I said. "What's wrong? Is everything okay down there?"

"I in Vermont, too," Alfonso said. I could picture his big smile.

"What do you mean, Alfonso?"

"I in Vermont, Bob. I sitting in the walk-in cooler. It jus' like Vermont."

I hung up and we all spent a few minutes imagining Alfonso bundled up in the walk-in cooler and talking about how bad we felt that he couldn't come on the trip. Then, just as everyone was settling in for a morning at home, we introduced them to the benefits of long underwear and headed out to a nearby hill with plastic sleds and flying saucers.

And there we all stood at the top of the hill. Nobody made a move. Mel and I reminded ourselves that they'd never even seen a sled before and needed some instruction. I jumped on a flying saucer and flew down the hill, headfirst and screaming for everyone to follow. I looked up from the bottom. Nobody moved.

Mel pointed over to another hill where some children were sledding up a storm. That seemed to do the trick.

"Man, look at those little kids," Ozzie said. "Come, Hughes. We goin' down together."

With Hughes and Ozzie leading the pack, there was no stopping them. Sledding became a contact sport as they held one another's hands and legs from sled to sled. First they were on their stomachs, then their backs. Sometimes they went alone and sometimes they piled on top of one another. By the end of the morning they were trying to figure out how they could introduce sledding as a sport to Anguilla.

King Arthur Flour is a wonderful company that happens to be based in our little town of Norwich. In addition to making some of the finest flour in the world, they also have a cooking school, bakery, and kitchen shop. When we told them we were bringing the whole crew from the restaurant up to visit, they asked if we'd stop by so everyone could sign some books.

We pulled into the parking lot and Mel ran ahead to announce our arrival. As soon as she saw the front door, I saw her stop dead in her tracks. She waved frantically for all of us to hurry. I couldn't imagine what was going on but urged everyone to speed things up. After a huge lunch at a local tavern, we were all moving a little slowly.

Mel had trouble getting in the door with the crowd inside. She ushered the staff through what turned out to be more than 120 people. They'd come to meet the characters whom they've grown to love from our books. Our staff had a fan club and didn't even know it. Their fans had read about them and couldn't wait to welcome them to Vermont. We had no idea so many people would be there, and it took a moment to collect our thoughts and figure out what to do next. Our staff was stunned and looked to us for some kind of direction.

The sight of ten Anguillians bundled up in turtlenecks, parkas, hats, gloves, and boots is something wondrous to behold. Surround them with over a hundred cheering fans applauding and reaching out to shake their hands, and it becomes a storybook dream.

"I feel like Michael Jordan," Miguel whispered to Mel. "All these people come just for us?"

"Just for you." Mel smiled.

"I can't believe this," Garrilin said. "These people have never even been to Anguilla."

We finally made our way to the front of the store and Cindy, the manager, stood up on a chair and thanked everyone for coming, then passed the show over to us.

"Where's Bug?" someone called from the crowd. "Yeah, where's Bug? And who's Lowell?" someone shouted.

Mel and I proceeded to introduce each member of our staff, giving a brief description and details about what he or she did in the restaurant. After answering every question, the twelve of us lined up behind the counter to sign books. Now, if you've ever been to an author signing, you know it's usually a fairly civilized event. An orderly line forms and the author signs one book at a time.

Not this time. Every one of our staff knows exactly on which page of each book his or her picture or name appears—and that's where they all wanted to sign their names. So for several hours we flipped pages back and forth in more than a hundred books, looking for the right page for each signature. Then, as everyone loosened up and began to feel more at home, simple autographs turned into longer messages. "Come see us in Anguilla so we can show you around," Ozzie wrote. And Garrilin inscribed "We love Vermont" in every book.

The next morning we woke up early, dressed for skiing, and drove to Killington. It had to be one of the coldest, windiest days in history. As we walked across the frozen parking lot to the lodge, I heard Hughes mumble under his breath, "I ain' goin' up there."

"Not me," Clinton added, looking up at the mountain.

I didn't say a word. Mel and I figured we'd just take it one step at a time. We handed out lift tickets and met the two instructors Killington had assigned to our group. Everyone lined up to be fitted for ski boots.

"This is what people wear on the moon," Alex told Clinton.

"This is not for me," Garrilin proclaimed.

"Nobody has to do this if they don't want to," Mel said. "But you'll be missing out on a lot of fun. I promise you. We wouldn't steer you wrong. Trust us."

Despite their apprehension, not a single person stayed behind. Their efforts were heroic. We'd invited some friends, planning to have one experienced skier for every staff member. We hoped that a one-to-one ratio would prevent any accidents.

As we were helping everyone put on their skis, the enormity of our situation hit me. Here we had ten people from a tropical island who'd never seen snow before. Not only were they outside in below-zero temperatures, but they were on skis, for goodness sake. What had we done?

Mel glided up alongside Garrilin, helping her up after she'd fallen over while following the instructor's lead to the flat beginner's area. I watched the two of them struggle as Garrilin regained her balance, fully expecting her to turn around and go back to the lodge. Instead, she raised her poles in the air and screamed, "I'm skiing!"

Except for Lowell's minor run-in with a giant tree—from which he fully recovered after a minute of hysterical laughter— we had a triumphant day of skiing. Some were more daring than others, but everyone gave it a try and everyone had a story to tell. At the end of the day we piled aboard the gondola, without skis, to see the top of the mountain. Once on top, the wind died down and for a moment we were in wonderland. The highest point in Anguilla is Crocus Hill, which tops off at 212 feet. Killington Peak is more than four thousand feet high and we felt like we were on top of the world. Miguel and Alex led everyone up the trail to the radio tower, which boasts views in all directions. The tree boughs were weighed down with heavy piles of snow; it seemed impossible that they hadn't broken off. We took dozens of pictures for the restaurant scrapbook.

A morning of snowmobiling was our last big adventure. After a brief lesson, we donned helmets and zoomed through the woods and across the fields of Vermont. We flew over bumps and raced one another past hunting cabins and rushing streams.

All talk of frozen eyeballs and dead car batteries was forgotten. Mel and I had accomplished our mission. We'd wanted to thank them for opening their hearts and letting us into their world on that faraway strip of sand in the Caribbean. Finally we'd been able to reciprocate.

When the American Eagle plane touched down in Anguilla, we overheard Ozzie saying as he looked out the window, "We back on the rock."

Remember

Do

Learn as much as you can about whatever it is you are considering.

Remember that living what you love is about more than money.

Fill your life and work with passion.

Don't

Assume that a lack of money will prevent you from living a meaningful life.

Discount the idea of taking baby steps instead of jumping in all at once.

Procrastinate.

Don't be afraid to go
out on a limb.
To take a risk. To fail.
Even to start over again.

Live What You Love.

remember

Buried Treasure

One Case Free with One

One of the wonderful rewards of living a life you love is the joy of remembering the life you lived—and are living. Our past is filled with tears of both joy and disappointment. The houses, the businesses, the cars, the products, and the cakes come and go. But the memories remain. That "history" contains your examination of little threads and big patterns, your application of the Big 4, your exercise of self-trust and personal adjustment, and your daily acts of commitment. Every day becomes a treasure. Every day remembered brings a rush as you recall your insistence upon your dream and the search for meaning. Each day is loved because it felt right and was extraordinary in the smallest details.

Join us. As in our writing of *Live What You Love*, look to your past and remember what you have loved about your life. Collect your stories—in writing, in conversation, in photographs—in your memory. Think about their little threads and big patterns. Value your memories of PASSION, PEOPLE, LOCATION, and MONEY. Share with others your history of self-trust and commitment. Celebrate the dreams, the searches, and the treasures of your life.

The remembering will bring you joy. It will renew your enthusiasm for a life that you love. You show yourself that you are in control of your time and your life. By looking at your past, you will understand yourself better. When you take the time to remember, you increase the value of your past experiences and cultivate your desire to live more moments to be treasured. Remembering honors the life that you love. Active remembering encourages an active and deliberate living.

Listen to your heart,
use your head, and
don't underestimate
the power of passion.

Buried Treasure

January 1983

We glared at the sign as we parked beneath it: "National Bank of New Hampshire—Serving You Since 1878." The thermometer in its center read −24°. "Serving *who* since 1878?" I mumbled.

"They didn't do anything wrong," Mel said. "We were the ones who borrowed all that money at two points over prime. It's the federal government that made interest rates soar to twenty-one and a half percent. I think the Federal Reserve put Kid's Connection out of business."

Ushered into the bank president's office, we were received with a greeting that felt as chilly as the January air outside. "I'm afraid we won't be able to release the lien on your house until you pay off the balance of your two-hundred-thousand-dollar loan," said Michael White, president. Looking down, he paused and reexamined that day's printout detailing our account, while busily punching in numbers on his adding machine. "You have an outstanding balance of three thousand six hundred fifty-seven dollars and twenty-two cents, including interest, as of today. How do you plan to take care of that?"

"Well, we sold every last fixture we owned as well as our delivery van, and I think we have enough here to settle our debt," Mel answered. "Would you mind telling me again exactly how much we owe?" Mr. White tore off the adding machine's tape and slid it across the desk as Mel pulled out our worn green vinyl bank bag and began carefully counting out money. After counting out all the bills, she reached back into the green bag and dug around the bottom for twenty-two cents in change, finally coming up with a quarter, which she carefully placed on the last stack of bills.

"Thank you," said Mr. White. "What are you going to do now?"

"I don't know," I said. "We'll figure something out." I looked at Mel, trying to be reassuring, knowing we were both scared to death.

"Thank you." Mel's voice started to tremble as she choked back tears. We both shook hands with Michael White and left.

Outside the snow squeaked under our boots and the wind sliced through our coats. I put my arms around Mel, no longer able to hold back her tears. "We'll get through this," I whispered, trying to sound convincing. We stood in the bank parking lot, arms around each other, for a long, frozen moment before finally climbing into the car.

We drove along in silence each lost in our own despair. And of course it was Mel, always the first to return to practicalities, who broke our reverie. She suddenly stopped crying and, reaching into the green bank bag, pulled out all of the remaining money and started counting it. "We've only got about four thousand dollars left and I'm not going to let anyone take it away from us. We've closed our three children's furniture stores, we've broken three retail leases, we have yet to hear back from any of the landlords, and we still owe money to several suppliers. I'm worried that someone will come after the house. We're hiding this money no matter what happens. This four thousand dollars isn't going to make a bit of difference to anyone and as long as it's hidden, we'll have something to get by on until we figure out our next step."

It's not easy digging a hole in frozen Vermont ground, but with the help of a pickaxe, we managed to get down about a foot. We put the money into several plastic bags to keep it dry and placed them into a gray metal box, thinking it would keep out mice. We carefully set our nest egg into the hole and covered it with the same frozen dirt we'd worked so hard to unearth. Stepping back, we turned to each other and smiled: we'd chosen to bury our treasure under the slide on Jesse's swing set so we'd remember the exact spot once it was covered with snow.

Once back inside, we played the messages on the answering machine, and all but one were from landlords trying to collect rent on spaces we no longer occupied. "We need a plan," Mel said. "We're going to get through this, but only if we don't sit around feeling sorry for ourselves. If it had been a different time, we would probably still be in business. Things just didn't work out that way. I'll always remember the line of customers that ran the length of the shopping center during our going-out-of-business sale. Each of them stood for hours waiting to buy anything they could find. And don't forget, we had to end the sale a day early because we didn't have a single item left to sell. I love living in Vermont but it's clear that the local market is too small and conservative to support any business except those dealing in necessities. And I don't think we have any interest in selling gasoline or toothpaste, do you?"

"You're right. We need to figure out how we can live here and create products that will sell in Boston and New York," I said. "Maybe we could start another Ben and Jerry's. We could call it Bob and Mel's."

"We can't do that," Mel said. "Nobody needs another Vermont ice cream. But some other food product might work—something besides maple syrup."

"Why don't we bottle a few of your great salad dressings?" I asked. "We could still use the name Bob and Mel's."

"I think the name should be more sophisticated, a Vermont version of Crabtree and Evelyn. We could make all kinds of food products like salad dressings, mustards, dessert sauces, marinades, and whatever else fits," Mel quickly shot back.

I could tell that Mel was getting excited and her enthusiasm set my mind racing. She was correct, the name "Bob and Mel's" simply wasn't right. That's when I had a brilliant idea. "Let's call it Blanchard & Blanchard!"

"What about Blanchard & Blanchard and Son?" Mel asked. "You know Jesse will want to help, so why not put his name on the label? It'll be much more fun if it's all three of us!" And so our specialty food company was born.

Jumping into high gear was the only way we knew how to go, and with few financial options, it was probably our only choice. So we proceeded, carefully spending our four-thousand-dollar treasure on glass bottles and cooking supplies. Mel spent the next several months developing recipes while I designed labels and managed to keep the wolves from our door by working as a carpenter.

I'd found a job with a construction crew that was rebuilding a burned-out house. The day I started work, they'd just begun putting on a new roof. It was impossible to hold a roofing nail with my gloves on, yet the nails froze to my fingers if I took the gloves off. It was colder work than you could ever imagine. Every morning I'd gather up my tools, pack my lunch pail with four peanut butter sandwiches, and set off to the job site wearing long underwear, wool pants, and coveralls. Every night I returned home cold, tired, and smelling like ashes. Mel sent me to shower the minute I walked into the house.

But the time passed quickly. In just over four months, we'd tested hundreds of recipes, built a trade show booth, and worked our way through dozens of labels and brochure designs. And finally we were ready to launch our new business. We'd shipped cartons of samples, along with our new booth, to the Gourmet Products Show in San Francisco. The show opened with Mel, Jesse, and me standing in our booth, full of excitement, pride, and determination; we'd worked hard, we had worked together, and we'd loved every minute of it. We weren't about to fail now.

For four days we handed out thousands of samples of our dressings and dessert sauces and talked to hundreds of food buyers, all of whom had come to San Francisco searching for new products. In those four days we learned more about the specialty food business than we could have ever been taught.

By the end of the show we had confirmed orders from Bloomingdale's, Macy's, and dozens of specialty stores all over the country, and we returned to Vermont with sales reps in fourteen states and purchase orders totaling over thirty-five thousand dollars in sales. Only then did it dawn on us that we had nothing but a blender and a large stockpot, and a lot of cooking to do.

Once again we drove to the National Bank of New Hampshire, but this time the sign outside registered a sunny 63°. It was a good omen. We presented Michael White our stack of purchase orders and talked him through our handwritten business plan. Mr. White listened carefully and spent several minutes poring over all of our paperwork. To our delight, he agreed to lend us enough money to buy several commercial blenders, drums of olive oil, and barrels of vinegar.

Spring was returning to New England. We weren't out of the woods yet but we were heading down a new, hopeful road. ✦

One Case Free with One
April 1989

Has there ever been something you'd love to do, but couldn't quite put all the pieces together to make it happen? Did it either seem so far-fetched or just too overwhelming to seriously consider? That happens to us all the time. Before we moved to the Caribbean, we'd go on tropical vacations and daydream about life under palm trees. We would talk about what it would be like to abandon Vermont's frigid winters and become part of an entirely new community. We wondered what it would be like to live year-round in Anguilla.

At first we dismissed the idea as wild and romantic. "Who on earth moves to the Caribbean?" we asked. But the subject of moving to paradise started popping up in our conversation more often—and the more we talked about it the less crazy it seemed. We began to meet people who had already done it and offered all kinds of helpful information.

We understood that transforming our pipe dream into reality would take careful planning, and that making a decision wasn't going to be easy, especially since our specialty-food company was growing quickly. Life wasn't bad: we were working together, earning a good living, and loved Vermont. But the pressures of a growing business were beginning to feel like a huge weight on our shoulders and it wouldn't shake off. Our partners' vision of the company's future was radically different from ours, and we found ourselves spending more time looking at income statements and balance sheets than creating new products and innovative marketing plans. We didn't dislike what we were doing, but the sparkle was gone. Our jobs had fallen into the "not so bad" trap.

The last straw came unexpectedly. Bob called one afternoon from Cincinnati shortly after meeting with a buyer from Food Stop supermarkets. Food Stop stores had done very well with a fifty-store test of our salad dressings and the buyer regaled Bob with his explanation of how the supermarket business operates. He told Bob about a recent battle waged by two spice companies for exclusive product placement in Food Stop stores. While each side fought hard, the East Indies Spice Company ultimately triumphed after they paid Food Stop full price for Island Bay's inventory. Once they owned Island Bay's product, the East Indies Spice Company arranged to have it all destroyed, filling Food Stop's shelves with their own merchandise—at no cost to Food Stop! Bob looked at the man incredulously, worried that he was about to ask us to do the same thing. Did this guy think we would buy Food Stop's inventory of Kraft dressings just to replace it with thousands of free cases of our own?

Bob sighed with relief as the buyer assured him that our situation was different. He knew we were a small company, he said, and he'd never ask to do anything like that. By the end of the meeting, Bob was told that getting our dressings onto the shelves in twelve hundred Food Stop stores would be no problem. All we had to do was give them one free case for every one purchased. After some quick calculating Bob figured this "bargain" would cost us a mere seven hundred thousand dollars! Throughout his dealings with Food Stop, Bob sensed that the products themselves, their quality and packaging, had no bearing on Food Stop's decision to carry them or on the deal itself. Just give them the money and the products would be allowed on the shelves.

Bob talked a mile a minute on the phone that afternoon, and it was clear to me that he'd made his final supermarket sales call. We spent the next weekend thinking long and hard about our life. We didn't fit in this world of wheeling and dealing; it was time to make a change. But how?

We tossed around countless ideas—everything from redefining our current roles within the company to finding jobs someplace else that would allow us to use more of our creative skills. As we considered each option, our dream of moving to Anguilla became more and more appealing.

Shortly after the Food Stop meeting, Anguilla became the most frequently used word in our house. We spent all our free time talking about how leaving our current world behind and moving to Anguilla would impact our lives. We covered every imaginable detail, trying to be realistic about how our decision might affect the world around us—family, friends, coworkers, weather, money, medical care, risk, security. Finally we reached the point where our dream of moving to the Caribbean was so compelling we'd lost all interest in doing our jobs. It was time to come up with a plan of action.

Remember

Do

Be honest with yourself.

Balance your personal priorities with your career goals.

Consider how much passion is in your life now and think about whether it's enough.

Don't

Allow others to decide how you live your life.

Be a pessimist.

Give up.

Never say no to a great idea.
Everything
is worth a shot because

anything is possible.

Afterword: *Live What You Love*

There can be a sensible, predictable path through life: We had plans for it early on. We told ourselves where we wanted to go and how we wanted to get there. We even set forth timelines, which we expected to follow obediently.

Then, it seems, the world said to us, *you people will be bored silly with that road.* And so along came Jesse's premature birth. And away went our plans and in came our complete surrender to the unknown. We replaced time lines and conventional choices with curiosity, dreams, and combinations of options that were perfect for us. If life could turn so quickly, we would just dance a little faster. If plans could crumble so dramatically, we would make sure that no matter what happened we'd be driven by our passion and the people and places we love.

Was it nonsense to step outside the lines of a usual life? To be honest, we really didn't have a choice. It was a gift from the world, in retrospect, and we could not stamp it RETURN TO SENDER. We were forced into an unusual life, and along the way we realized that love is the most stable, reliable, and trustworthy condition in the universe. When nothing else lasts, when nothing else is true, there is love.

We thank our lucky stars every day that the world kicked us off the predictable path and into a life we love. And we found the courage not to wait on the world to give us this gift again. We can still choose to step out of the usual and into the unusual at any point in time. You know which one we prefer. In fact, the more comfortable and rewarding we found the unusual path, the more determined we became to wander across new boundaries and follow new dreams.

It makes us sad to see so many wonderful people secretly feeling that they have failed when the sensible, usual path through life just doesn't work out—when they get knocked off it, just as we did. We struggled in our early years to see that being pushed off the traditional path did not mean we'd lost our way. In fact, that's when our journey actually began.

For us, living what we love was not a plan—it was a transformative experience that revealed itself to us. We just gave over to it—as anyone can. We never dreamed that living what we love would end up as life in Anguilla, as inspiration to others, or as the little book you are holding.

Looking back, we now know that the day we met changed us forever. We fell in love deeply and instantly, and never wanted anything else but a life together (there's no other way to survive living in a VW bus for months on end!). Our love for each other gives us the courage to confront the deep vulnerability each time we say *what if*. Without this love, we never would have made it through Jesse's birth, never would have opened our first store, never would have moved to Anguilla. The honesty required to really live what we love gives us permission at any point in time to say, *Wait . . . we need to change.*

That is how we went to—and came back from—California. It is how we built a home in Vermont. Did we fail in our West Coast adventure? Did we abandon our Anguilla family? No! We lived deep in the middle of love—and that is what allowed us to find the next story and make the next choice.

Blanchard & Blanchard would not have happened if we had stayed in California. So "re-deciding" on where we wanted to live took us to the right place in the end. If we had not built our home in Vermont, the staff at Blanchard's Restaurant would not have discovered how deeply they trust one another, or how much we trust them. If we had not planned an impossible ski trip, our Anguilla family would never have shown us what snow looks like through new eyes. Love made all of these things happen—but our willingness to live it out loud and trust its unpredictable changes is why all of our dreams have come true.

Whether married, partnered, or single, you can live what you love. You just have to get over the jitters and let your dreams show you the way. Tie your kite to reality and check your gut whenever it says, "Hey, wait!" Take action when the time is right and remember and treasure what life shows you . . . but don't ever stand in the way of what you really love.

As far as we can tell, dreams are nothing more than love trying to take wing and soar. Imagine for just a moment the thrilling, distracting, wonderful, unusual sensation of new love—of first love. You immediately begin dreaming of life together, of where you will go, of what life will mean for the two of you. We live in that moment every day. We fall in love with new ideas, new opportunities, and new places all the time. And because we trust love, we live it. Who are we to say no to love or to crush a dream that wants to live? It isn't that hard to give yourself over to it. You just have to say yes to life and to love. People may lie, cheat, or be insincere—we've seen all of this before—but love itself will never lead you astray.

If we had not given ourselves over to living what we love . . . well, who knows where we would be? We know with certainty that life would not feel rich, rewarding, and exciting. We probably never would have heard of Anguilla. But we did . . . and here we are. We trusted it then, and we trust it now.

Over time we've learned to see the patterns of our life emerge before our eyes. We trust that there is a reason things happen the way they do, that there's meaning in the little things, that living a life we love has a bit of magic to it. We trust where we are going because we are together. Just like our old '49 Dodge carried our dreams to Peanie and our very first store, we're trusting our old '92 Mercury right now to take us toward what is next. Who knew our dream car would have no hubcaps?

And so, as always, forward we go. Today, one of the world's most famous and respected movie stars is sitting in the backseat. We're going to meet the CEO of a national retail giant, a friend who dines with us in Anguilla each year. Both of them would like to partner with us on a new project here on the island. *How did we get here . . . what did we do . . . is this dream real?*

Once again real estate—place—is our starting point. Like California, like Vermont, if it feels right, we'll all know. Right now it's just a dream. The land alone costs many millions of dollars—and we certainly do not have that amount buried under a swing set somewhere. First things first, though: We love the idea and we love the land. Passion, people, and place all seem to be in order. Now it's just the detail of the money. Then the Big 4 will be aligned.

This dream—this next chapter, unwritten, of *Live What You Love*—may be the biggest disappointment of our lives or the most exciting adventure yet. Who knows? We'll trust that whatever does happen is what should happen.

With each dream we've ever had, we say it out loud—allowing our words to have the breath of inspiration behind them: *Now we are working on our latest dream, a Blanchard's Hotel and Resort.* Will it happen? Don't know. If it does, will it succeed? Don't know. Do we have any idea how to build a hotel in the Caribbean? No. But as with our house in Vermont, we assume it's done from the ground up. So that's where we are starting . . . with the ground. Our dream is tied to earth. Maybe it will fly.

All we know for sure is this: At this moment we are together, living what we love. The sun shines today. The water dances. The breeze sings a song.

The windows are down and we are bouncing on duct-tape-covered seats, heading to the sea, ready again to jump in together. Wonder what it will feel like? Wonderful? Unusual? Yes, even after all these years.

Will you live a life you love? We hope so. Anyone with a heart filled with dreams is already halfway there. Take a deep breathe. Jump in. Life is to be lived and to be loved.

Do you find yourself counting
the days until the weekend?

Life doesn't
have to be that way.

Acknowledgments

Writing this book was one of the most difficult projects we have ever tackled. We couldn't have written it so quickly, and wouldn't have enjoyed the experience nearly so much, without the support, advice, and encouragement of everyone who has believed in *Live What You Love* from its inception. Our love and gratitude extends to everyone who helped make this book a reality.

To Patrick Davis: Your remarkable vision, humbling intelligence and unflappable belief in this book have been miraculous. *Live What You Love* became a much better book thanks to your encouragement, humor, and guidance; any remaining flaws are entirely of our own making. You are our heaven-sent angel and we thank you from the bottom or our hearts.

We also thank your brilliant team at Patrick Davis Partners who have all been cheerful, supportive, and understanding. And our special thanks to Jennifer Brinkmann, Lisa Tilt, Kristin Dormeyer, Michele Parrish, Becky Coulter, and Chad Boyd for your help and encouragement.

Thank you to the whole gang at Sterling. Extra thanks to Steve Magnuson, our fantastically talented editor, whose insights and unfailing support from start to finish kept us writing through many drafts. Thanks for sticking by us. It was more work than any of us had envisioned but we sure had fun, didn't we? And thanks to Steve Riggio, Charlie, Andy, Leigh Ann, Rena, Vivian, Emma, and Jennifer for welcoming us into the Sterling family with such open arms.

To Kiku Obata, Eleanor Safe, and Joe Floresca: Your graphic genius and creative vision have added a superb and colorful new layer to our text, imbuing each page with astonishing visual energy. You have made *Live What You Love* come to life in Technicolor surpassing our greatest expectations. Your talent is unparalleled and we look forward to working together again soon. We've had too much fun to stop now.

And a big thank you to John Murphy, who came for dinner

and ended up working. Thanks, John! We appreciate all of your input and advice. To Michael Raymond, we send our thanks for your clear and thoughtful review of the text, which magnificently saved the day at *Live What You Love*'s final hour of a tight schedule. And we are forever indebted to Michael Carlisle, without whom we might never have become authors. Thank you, Michael.

To Lauren Shakely and Pam Krauss: A giant thanks for having enough faith in us to put corporate rules aside by courageously agreeing to simultaneously publish our cookbook with *Live What You Love*. *Cook What You Love* and *Live What You Love* will be forever linked in marriage.

To Annetta Hanna: We've said it before and will say it again—we can't imagine writing a book without you. Thanks for your keen editorial insight, sharp pencil, and continued friendship. This is not our last book together!

And with enormous gratitude, we send a big thank you to the people of Anguilla, particularly our staff at Blanchard's Restaurant: Lowell Hodge, Clinton Davis, Miguel Leverett, Renford "Bug" Gumbs, Ozzie Rey, Alex Smith, Huegel Hughes, Garrilin Nisbett, Alwyn Richardson, Tarah Baker, Alfonso Brooks, Rinso Hodge, Bootsie Gumbs, Samaro Richardson, and Joadi Romney. Without you, none of this would have been possible. Together, we all live what we love.

You've got to
take chances

for the things
you care about.

Photo Captions